SEMIOTEXT(E) ACTIVE AGENTS SERIES

Originally published as *Les mots et la terre*. © Librairie Arthème Fayard, 2006.
© This edition 2011 by Semiotext(e).

Published by Semiotext(e)
2007 Wilshire Blvd., Suite 427, Los Angeles, CA 90057
www.semiotexte.com

Special thanks to John Ebert and Marc Lowenthal.

Cover Photography: The Dead Sea, 1919. Courtesy Library of Congress.
Back Cover Photography: Olivia Grabowski-West.
Photographs on page 1 and 238–239: © 2010 Jorge Alberto Perez.
www.jorgealbertoperez.com
Design by Hedi El Kholti

ISBN: 978-1-58435-096-5
Distributed by The MIT Press, Cambridge, Mass. and London, England
Printed in the United States of America

THE WORDS AND THE LAND

ISRAELI INTELLECTUALS
AND THE NATIONALIST MYTH

Shlomo Sand

Translated by Ames Hodges

\<e\>

Contents

Where I Am Speaking From

*It follows that when we take up a work of history, our first con-
cern should be not with the facts which it contains but with the
historian who wrote it.*
— Edward H. Carr, *What Is History*, 1961.

*Intellectuals are always ready to leave their own game and their
own stakes out of play.*
— Pierre Bourdieu, *Sociology in Question*, 1994.

Every book is part autobiography. This is all the more true when
the book involves intellectuals. The author—sociologist, philosopher, journalist or historian—might not be eager to recognize this
fact, but denying it would be like producing a book with a con-
genital anomaly.

The present work is dedicated to Israeli intellectuals. As a
professor of history at the University of Tel Aviv and often engaged
in public debate in Israel, I felt the need to preface this book with
an "autobiographical confession" to tell readers where I am coming
from and the different temporal strata involved.

Growing Up

I was born at the end of 1946 in Linz, Austria. My parents were Polish Jews who fled the ruins of Europe after World War II and the murder of their parents. My birth in the town where Hitler grew up and where he dreamed, until the very end, of building a model city for the Third Reich was pure coincidence. Years later, during times of political discouragement, my birthplace was often a source of motivation: how ironic to give birth to a Jewish boy in the city of the defeated Führer's broken dreams! The irony did not stop there. Soon after my birth, my family moved to a "displaced persons" camp in Traunstein, near Munich. At the end of World War I, the area had served as camp for war prisoners and Corporal Hitler was one of the guards! We stayed in the camp at the foot of the Bavarian Alps for almost two years before emigrating to Israel at the end of 1948, when the last fighting was still in full swing.

On arriving in the "Holy Land," we were housed in Jaffa, in a one-room apartment that the owners had just abandoned. I spent my youth in the working-class neighborhoods of Jaffa in the 1950s and 60s; we always lived in small apartments left behind by Palestinian refugees who had fled to Gaza. My father, already a communist militant in Poland in the 1930s, remained dedicated until the end. From when I was very young, he always reminded me that we had taken someone else's home. We probably had no choice, since Europe had "spit us out" and we had nowhere else to go, but my father always said that, one day, we would have to pay the price for what had been taken from the Palestinians. He never said how we would pay, and I am not sure he knew.

My education in a communist family in the young State of Israel meant travelling through collective identities with two-sided baggage. In school, I was fed the Zionist order of time, while at home and in the communist youth movement I was taught history with a different intellectual texture. These two approaches probably contributed to a particular sensibility, one that some might call "twisted," but that left me less willing to accept without question the dominant representations of the past in Israel.

Before distinguishing between "Zionist time" and "communist time," I should mention that they shared several points. They were each based on an idea of progress and gave the impression of building a future life in a better world. They each replaced the cyclic and religious time that had probably been predominant in my grandparents' minds (at least as I imagine them, since I never had the chance to know them), and surely in the minds of their parents and grandparents.

While they each claimed a connection to socialism, Zionist time declared itself to be national while communist time was universalist. Each saw that the promise of redemption was underway. For Zionist time, liberation took place here, in the little "Israeli homeland"; for "communist time," it was in the "land of socialism." At first, I refused to see any contradiction between these two projects and could not understand the stubborn opposition to the "Reds." I remember enthusiastically participating in an impressive work at school that involved reconstructing, in plaster and paper, the draining of the Hula Valley, and around the same time, my excitement at hearing about the exalted creation of communes in China. In their own way, these two sensibilities gave me an insatiable desire to contribute to a redemption and it was only much later, and with some sadness, that I escaped the hold of their myths.

My greatest advantage over the non-communist youth of my generation was that I had the opportunity to meet Arab youths in the communist youth movement, one of whom, Mahmoud Moussa, became a close friend. Students in Israeli schools and the members of Zionist youth movements only rarely had the occasion to encounter young Palestinians: the concepts of Zionist time and identity did not include them. They promised national liberation, but only for Jews, in a political space that included the indigenous people, but only "by chance." I quickly saw the contradiction between the universal values proclaimed by Zionist socialism in the 1950s and 60s and the daily discrimination on a national and linguistic level that caused my friend, who wanted so badly to be Israeli, to suffer. I was lucky enough not to have experienced the contradictions between the universal values of communism and their practice in the Soviet Union and other "popular democracies." I remained one of the faithful for some time, albeit in the abstract.

I don't know if my existence in the shadow of this national-universal contradiction contributed to my lack of academic success. Adolescent angst and Jaffa's beautiful beaches, where I grew up, were also a considerable factor in this embarrassing mess. My early expulsion from high school brought my study of history to an end, at least in the formal structure of the public school system. I was bitter at the time, but later was able to see how it allowed me to pursue freely a variety of vocations, from literature and philosophy to history. As a young worker performing tasks that required no intellectual investment, I let my imagination roam free to escape the oppressive temporal and spatial confines. When I wasn't working, I indulged in a frenzy of reading to feed my imagination, in a desperate attempt to escape to other times and other places.

The June 1967 War brought me back to concrete history. The aggressiveness of the war brought the individual and the collective together by placing my life in danger (I was a young soldier sent into the fighting in Jerusalem). And a year later, the invasion of Czechoslovakia by the armies of the Warsaw Pact chased away the dreams of communism. These two events shook my linear view of history, causing the first serious doubts about the possibility of "historical progress." However, with the utopia of the New Left sweeping the world, and Israel basking in the unhealthy euphoria of the "Six Day War," I did not lose hope of playing my part in changing the world and joined the ranks of the far Left. The dream of the future that it offered was more attractive and pure than the communist world, even though it was politically much more shortsighted. What I took from my time with Matzpen (an extreme left-wing movement founded in 1962 by young anti-Stalinist dissidents from the Communist Party) was a more acute critique of grand, national syntheses and the first systematic confrontation with Zionist history. Matzpen was the first group, I believe, to have proposed the arguments that would later be called "Post-Zionist" by the Israeli press.

During my militant period with Matzpen, still a young worker and academic dilettante, I often suffered from the tyranny of the "historical knowledge" of the students and professors who participated in the movement. They acted like the founding members of a closed circle, and the siege mentality, combined with our awareness of the vast distance between our dreams and reality, gave our activities a frenetic aspect that dampened my last revolutionary impulses to change the course of history. At that point, I had no choice but to turn back to my study of history in a formal academic context.

Studying

To begin university studies, I first had to pass the Bagrut as an external candidate. My results were not good enough to open any doors other than the University of Tel Aviv's Faculty of Humanities. I first registered with the philosophy department, motivated by my fascination with a few Western philosophers and my "weakness" for theoretical debate. My thirst for knowledge of the past did not abate, and for the first time I felt the need to study it more systematically. However, cruel political disappointments and severe doubts about the rationality of human behavior made me apprehensive to confront the "real" parts of reality head-on. I thought that escaping into creative imagination would be better and turned to the literature department. The first problem came when I was called before the admissions committee: it was in 1971 and I was afraid my long hair and long collars might not be well received. I therefore turned to the Department of History. While we all know that specific circumstances do not have a direct impact on the "long term," they can be decisive turning points for individuals.

My intention was to combine studies of "general history" with the "history of the Jewish people," but the few courses I took in the latter discipline quickly revealed that it had nothing to offer me. A year later, I also dropped philosophy: a course with an impressive professor on Plato's *Republic* that did not require any knowledge of the political and social world of the Greek *polis* convinced me of the need to study texts in their context. To give a sense to concepts, even abstract ones, you have to know where they originate, and the places that are the subject and object of the discourse. I never gave up reading philosophy, and this reading has fed my historiographical thinking, but I prefer studying political and social theories in their specific historical contexts. My decision to study the intrigues of the past was influenced the most by the intellectual vivacity of the history department in the early 1970s. It was a very exciting department with professors from the margins of the political scene who were open to the daring historiographical sensibilities found in the history departments of Europe from Cambridge to Berlin.

After the period of intense activity with the communists and the leftists, I experienced student life in the history department as a kind of rebirth. The generosity and encouragement of the professors that I studied under was only rivaled by their extensive knowledge and talent. Some were very demanding, but well worth the effort. At first, after so many intellectually unbridled years, I had difficulty adapting to the rhythm of university study, especially since I also had to work for a living. But I quickly got used to it and was able to obtain some scholarships. After the trauma of my expulsion from high school, after the Stalinist yoke of the youth movement and after the cloistered life of Matzpen, this new experience was liberating and healthy therapy.

The October 1973 War broke the thread of these years of idyll. After the 1967 War, I had fulfilled my annual obligations as a reserve soldier by serving as a combat medic. Each year, I went to the occupied territories in a state of distress, even though the popular insurrection of the Palestinians had not yet occurred and colonization had not increased its pace. The "Yom Kippur War" found me in active service as a reservist in the Sinai desert. At the end of the fighting, I decided never to wear a uniform again. The sight of dogs scavenging the shredded corpses of Egyptian soldiers in the sand left me profoundly shaken. The thought that I could have died in a stupid war caused by mediocre politicians "on my side" eliminated the last vestiges of social conformity left in me.

The refusal of Golda Meir and her government on the Left to respond to the obvious signals for peace coming from Anwar El Sadat before the hostilities began and the number of victims caused by their blindness convinced me to seek a change of air.

Leaving

After finishing my undergraduate degree, as a Yiddish speaker who had taken German for two years, I thought I could go to Frankfurt to study in the language of Kant and Marx, but a grant from the French government tipped the scale in favor of Paris. I was fascinated by the "City of Light." The vestiges of May '68 and the study grant that allowed an extended stay in Europe were an irresistible attraction. I enrolled at the University of Paris-VIII Vincennes. Under the direction of Madeleine Rebérioux, and with the generous and warm help of my friend Michel Bilis, I finished a Master's thesis on "Jean Jaurès and the National Question."[1] I had done everything I could to distance myself from Israel, but I could not stop thinking about the big secret hidden in the idea of national identity.

My encounters in the French academic world were not particularly reassuring: the professors were sincere and welcoming, but as an Israeli I did not feel comfortable, especially around students at Vincennes in the 1970s. For many French leftists at the time, contact with an Israeli was an unpardonable offense. The fact that I was not a Zionist did not seem to help, because I continued to define my identity as an Israeli and defend the State of Israel's right to exist. Marxist-Leninists of all types and Arab students were not ready to accept this nuance and preferred to keep their distance. Going back today to read the verbal gymnastics employed by many leftists at the time to exalt the largest "popular democracy" in the world, and who now use no less hasty generalizations to vaunt the merits of the "only democracy" in the Middle East is both amusing and disturbing.

From that point on, I stopped claiming to be an anti-Zionist. For the far Left in Europe, unlike its Israeli counterpart, anti-Zionism meant the negation of the State of Israel's right to sovereign existence, as I quickly understood at Vincennes. But I continue to waver, since I consider myself now to be "non-Zionist" and no longer react when people label me a "post-Zionist historian." The minimal sense that we can give the term "Zionism" today implies the recognition of the State of Israel as a Jewish State or the State of the Jews. While that meaning justifiably made sense in 1948 when hundreds of thousands of refugees were still wandering in Europe without safe haven, support for Israel as a Jewish State today and not as an Israeli State carries with it an essentially non democratic aspect. As I note in this book, the Israeli Minister of the Interior defines 25% of the country's citizens as "non Jewish." Given that it is impossible for them to join the "Jewish State" in a voluntary and secular manner, despite the fact that they have the right to vote, the Jewish State, in principle and in fact, is not the State of all its citizens. According to the spirit of its fundamental laws, Israel belongs to those people in the world who consider themselves Jewish, even if they are not persecuted, and not to its Arab or other citizens who speak Hebrew and participate in the Israeli economy and culture. As a democrat and a defender of republican values, I cannot accept the *de facto* situation in Israel today.

The difference between the ethnic-exclusive definition of nationality inherited from Central and Eastern Europe and the civil-cultural definition developed in the West began to become clearer in my mind—although not completely—when I finished my work on Jaurès. There is no doubt that engaging the thought of this Socialist leader contributed greatly to refining my republican ideas on belonging to a nation.

In 1977, after finishing my Master's thesis, I decided to leave Paris-VIII for the École de hautes études en sciences sociales (EHESS: School for Advanced Studies in Social Sciences). I believed that it would be less affected by the slow decay of Leftism in all its forms and I could focus more on my studies. The school was closer to where I was keeping residence and I knew it was highly esteemed by Israeli universities. My first, decisive contact was with Georges Haupt, who later became the adviser on my doctoral thesis. During our first meeting, he convinced me to abandon my initial project (anti-positivism in French socialism) and turn to Georges Sorel and his relationship with Marxism. My prior encounter with Sorel had already had a significant impact on my intellectual and professional development and merits a quick digression.

Meeting

Before arriving in Paris, I was only familiar with a few of Sorel's works. This controversial figure first drew my attention after Isaiah Berlin's visit to the University of Tel Aviv in 1973. The erudite Oxford scholar chose "The Philosophy of Violence" as the topic of his talk and proposed a theoretical model for the possibility of a shift by young revolutionaries from the far Left to the nationalist Right. Sorel, who began his career as an admirer of theoretical

Marxism, later became a fierce defender of revolutionary syndicalism and at the end of his life was an adept of Mussolini and fascism, according to the information available at the time. For Isaiah Berlin, his fate could be shared by the leftists of the early 1970s, some of whom had already turned to terrorist action: their future struggles could lead them to the Right and into moral nihilism.[2]

Coming from the far Left, I was curious to learn about the new political abyss opening in front of me, especially since I was completely disoriented by the collapse of this Left in Europe and the United States. I started doing research on Sorel and the writing dedicated to him, primarily in English translations, to get a better understanding of his thought and its strange and extreme shifts. I gathered enough material for a presentation on "Sorel, the Source of His Fascist Thinking" for one of my final seminars at the University of Tel Aviv; it was well-received by my professor, Walter Laqueur. The connection between the extreme Left and the extreme Right, leading inescapably to totalitarianism, has always been part of the historical imagination of many neo-liberal scholars, and they gladly welcomed the image of Sorel at this crossroads.

The sole problem with the analogy established by Isaiah Berlin, which I was not aware of at the time, was that it was based on an imprecise evaluation of the two compared terms: as we know today, the exalted extreme Left of the 1960s did not shift to the extreme Right and did not lead to the emergence of a new fascism. My later study of fascism in Italy and Nazism in Germany revealed that only a very small number of intellectuals from the revolutionary Left rallied to the nationalist Right, when compared to the influx of neo-liberals, moderate democrats and solid conservatives who supported these mass movements (either out of conformism or nationalism).

In 1977, around the time when I met Georges Haupt, the translation of Antonio Gramsci's writings was reaching an end and I began to master French while reading them. Sorel's presence at the point of origin for many of Gramsci's most important ideas struck me and raised several questions. The Italian communist philosopher saw Sorel as the most important theorist since Marx and criticized the fascists who claimed him.[3] Isaiah Berlin and many Anglo-Saxon neo-liberal analysts (as well as François Furet in his book *The Passing of an Illusion*)[4] saw Sorel as a source of fascism and firmly stated that he had supported the Blackshirts. It is true that Mussolini sometimes mentioned Sorel's name along with Goethe and Garibaldi as one of his intellectual inspirations. Yet Gramsci, perhaps the most virulent anti-fascist in all of Italy, and his friend the radical neo-liberal Piero Gobetti also declared themselves to be "Sorelians."

By chance, Sorel's correspondence with a long line of Italian intellectuals was discovered, which is why Haupt suggested that I work on this subject. This surprising and original thinker's relationship to Marxism and to myths in history, in the context of the intellectual debates at the turn of the previous century, seemed engaging enough for me to pursue as the topic of my thesis. And so I began to look at Sorel again.

As I began research on this "muddle head," as Lenin once called him, more than sixty essays and university theses had already been dedicated to him. For an Israeli with a shaky grasp of French to take on this subject may have seemed arrogant or pretentious. Especially since Sorel, a retired civil engineer, had such a vast knowledge of science and Christianity that I felt like I was diving into a bottomless pit. My own baggage of knowledge and methodology from the University of Tel Aviv was like a life preserver at the hardest times. I finished my thesis, it was published,[5] and I became a "Sorel specialist."

I was able to use newly discovered documents and a rereading of long-forgotten published works to raise doubts about the idea that Sorel had finished his life as an admirer of fascism. Unlike his friend Benedetto Croce, who supported Mussolini like many Italian neo-liberals at least until 1925, Sorel felt a strong aversion to the Blackshirts until his death and considered their leaders to be dangerous, unstable individuals. Even in his most theoretical positions, I could not find the slightest trace of "fascist thought"—see for example his violent critique of the increasing power of the State and his dislike of anonymous masses gathered behind their loud leaders. His irresponsible political language, his unstable, spiteful personality and in particular his disparaging remarks about Jews after the Dreyfus Affair were very unpleasant but they helped prevent me from identifying with him. At the same time I realized that a historian should follow the evolution of ideas from Mussolini to Sorel and not from Sorel to Mussolini; from Robespierre to Rousseau not from Rousseau to Robespierre; from Lenin to Marx and not from Marx to Lenin. The wide-spread and comfortable illusion is to think that experienced politicians are inspired by erudite thinkers and "influenced" by their ideas. It took me some time to realize that they use their sophisticated and pragmatic selectivity to pick only those aspects that might be useful to them to "make history." As Lucien Goldmann noted, the verb "to influence" has no meaning in itself. It has to be explained anew each time.

The lesson I took from my doctoral thesis is that in the domain of ideas, as in any other domain of history, you cannot make any progress without the tools of sociology. Accepting this principle, and the sociology of knowledge, led me to look more closely at questions related to the status of intellectuals, the relationships of force between them, the conditions of production of their works and their position in the political arena. These subjects brought me to the work of Pierre Bourdieu, and because I studied history and not sociology, I started attending Jacques Julliard's classes at the EHESS at the end of the 1970s.

Luckily for me, Jacques Julliard was also interested in Sorel through his deep interest in labor autonomy at the time. Despite the distance between our political sensibilities, I was drawn by his theoretical approach and boundless curiosity. He was brave enough to give me his professional trust by having me participate in the publication of the acts of a conference on Sorel.[6] He also introduced me to François Furet and Jacques Revel, who offered the chance to teach at the EHESS. As a chair of Judaism Studies had just been created, my first class had the theme "Zionism and Socialism." Through the class, I came to reexamine the approaches to Jewish nationalism by Ber Borochov, Bernard Lazare and Martin Buber. I was able to close the circle that had begun with my Master's thesis on Jaurès. But I had learned how to take the measure of the questions raised by nationalism now that I was free of my prior revolutionary political illusions. My encounter with the author of *Illusions of Progress* changed my perception of historical time.

Julliard tried to convince me to stay in France and continue my work on Sorel, with the goal of creating a critical edition of his writing, but the attractive offer of a teaching position in the history department of the University of Tel Aviv brought me back to Israel. To be honest, the same intellectual and mental conflict that had caused me to leave the "Jewish democracy" a decade earlier played a role in my decision to return. I believed for a time that public reaction to the Lebanon War had made it possible to create a serious political and theoretical opposition to both occupation and the ethnocentric nationalism at the base of Zionist culture. Unlike Albert Camus, who yearned for sun-filled lands but preferred to live in Paris, I missed Israeli warmth, both in its climate and its people. I also wanted to move closer to my parents, who remained emigrants until their last days. They never felt Israeli, as I did, despite spending a majority of their lives in that harsh and torrid corner of the Middle East.

Returning

As I mentioned, I now teach at the University of Tel Aviv. I still dedicate most of my time to the cultural history of Europe and the West. After several years studying the political ideas and socio-history of intellectuals,[7] I recently turned to the mechanisms of cinema and its interactions with the modern era. During my stay at the EHESS, I met Marc Ferro, the founder of the discipline, and took an interest in his work on film. I hesitated for some time before deciding to study moving images, in large part to avoid ruining the pleasure of watching a movie. Yet pursuing research on modern political culture and its hegemonic ideologies while ignoring material on film would have been missing something vital. I then had the idea to tell the history of the 20th century through film; it became a book that was warmly received in Israel but harshly attacked in France by some of the admirers of the film *Shoah*.[8]

At first I was surprised by the violence of these critiques when I had only written three pages out of five hundred and twenty on Claude Lanzmann's film. Everyone has the right to criticize my analysis of a film, especially when my book was full of personal remarks and opinions that not everyone would share. I can also understand that the particular sensibility of French Jewish intellectuals in relation to the Shoah is different than my own, and I try to respect that difference. However, I found that the tone of Lanzmann's admirers and the tone of the film itself held something of the tendency that I refer to in the present book.

Continuing to take dividends from the capital of suffering of prior generations is a relatively common cultural phenomenon. It can be found in the intellectuals of the Third World who frequent Parisian salons and in the descendants of the Armenians, among Palestinian refugees and the descendants of French Jews. I admire the filmmakers of the 1950s like Alain Resnais, Gillo Pontecorvo and Armand Gatti who produced works of universal memory to shake heroic Europe from the comfort of forgetting at a time when the survivors of the extermination were neglected and sometimes disdainfully pushed aside. But I have serious reservations today about directors and intellectuals who continue to promote the uniqueness of the Jewish victims, making them the sole martyrs and forbidding any comparison with other victims.

My grandmothers, my grandfathers and my aunt were taken into the gas chambers (they were among the first deportees from the Lodz ghetto) and they were no more unique than other people. They were no better or worse than their non-Jewish neighbors. They never believed that they belonged to a chosen people and their death did not confer on them the status of chosen victims. Their executioners were the ones who wanted to portray them as unique and outside history or who were motivated by the will to dominate. It is important to remind all of those who refuse to see it that the uniqueness of the project of extermination was not the identity of its victims (or the identity of the collaborators) but in the awful efficiency of the assassins and the astonishing perversity of their crimes.

In my profession as a historian, I contribute directly and sometimes unintentionally to the collective memory. I feel a certain satisfaction in the fact that the "unconventional" murder of Jews, Gypsies and homosexuals has been taken out of the margins where the writing of European history had left it and that it has taken its place alongside the memory of the millions of other victims killed by more "conventional" means. But I also feel somewhat uneasy that death and land have become the primary instructors and guides of the Israeli national memory and that they are now the unique common marker for the modern Jewish identity.

In Israel and abroad, the agents of memory from many backgrounds work to remember and reconstitute the act of collective death but they dedicate little time to the pre-war Yiddish culture that disappeared in the tumult (in Israel, the history of Judeo-Arab culture has also been forgotten). For the memory of the Shoah, and without particular investment, it is easy to benefit from a moral surplus value and to quiet critics of the Israeli occupation.

I am well aware that this book will not please everyone. I am not sure whether Frederic Jameson, the American cultural critic, was right when he said that "history is what hurts," but I think that at least part of teaching contemporary history involves discomfort, since we are all involved.

This book has no intention of giving moral lessons and will never be a good book if it serves a particular political agenda. However, the quality of a discourse on history depends on the disturbing questions it raises and the sometimes slippery bridges it builds between past and present, between imagination and memory, bridges that are not always safe.

Intellectuals and the National Imagination

*The significance of the emergence of Zionism and the birth of
Israel is that the former marks the reimagining of an ancient religious community as a nation, down there among the other
nations—while the latter charts an alchemic change from wandering devotee to local patriot.*
— Benedict Anderson, *Imagined Communities*, 1983.

*Will it be possible to turn a citizen's group into a form of imag-
ined community to which its members feel like they belong? Can
democratic citizens create their own patriotism?*
— Azmi Bishara, Postscript to the Hebrew edition of
Imagined Communities, 1998.

These days we all know more or less who the "intellectuals" are.
They have been studied extensively and in France alone have been
the subject of dozens of essays in the last quarter of the 20th
century. From Régis Debray's pioneering work to the synthetic
dictionary by Jacques Julliard and Michel Winock,[1] intellectuals
and their status have become a well-defined area of research fed by

a variety of approaches from around the world. Yet there is no consensus on the use of the term "intellectual." Sociology uses it in a specific way and political history uses it in another. The word is sometimes a synonym of "intelligentsia" in reference to all those who earn their living producing and distributing cultural represen-tations and symbols. The concept can also be used to define producers of high culture who consciously create macro-ideologies and intervene in the public arena with a specific political discourse.

Unlike the times when the classic works of Julien Benda, Ray-mond Aron and Jean-Paul Sartre appeared,[2] the last quarter of the 20th century saw the development of a new research climate, permitting the necessary distance to study intellectuals, almost "from the outside." It became possible to approach intellectual groups as objects of research without falling into debates fed by passion, empathy or antipathy. It became possible to see how intel-lectuals defended ideals and ideologies to serve governments or various social groups, but also how they were motivated by specific collective interests and particular strategies of self-promotion.

The Anglo-Saxon world and other national cultures have also produced interesting work on intellectuals, from Lewis A. Coser to Russell Jacoby, including György Konrád and Iván Szelényi.[3] Their work did not contribute to the same systematic research or the same dramatic notoriety as the work of French scholars. In France, the "invention" of the intellectual dates from the end of the 19th century and the country of Voltaire and Zola has perfected the conceptualization and historicization of the field of research dedi-cated to intellectuals.

Theories related to nations and nationality have also developed and evolved over the last three decades. While a historian like Marc Bloch could write that "the texts make it plain that so far as France and Germany were concerned this [national] consciousness was already highly developed about the year 1100,"[4] this kind of historical evaluation became less acceptable after the early 1980s. The work by Benedict Anderson, Ernest Gellner and Eric Hobsbawm shook the foundations of traditional research on the national question, forming new, radical paradigms that overturned the basis of our understanding of the concept of "nation."[5] In this geopolitical space, the concept was formed and the first national consciousness was forged that revealed the deepest flaws in conventional historiography related to national identity. The *Encyclopedia of Nationalism* under the direction of Alexander Motyl was the crowning development of this field of research.[6]

There have also been incisive analyses of the development of nations outside the Anglo-Saxon world: essays by Anne-Marie Thiesse, Dominique Schnapper and Miroslav Hroch, for example, have made decisive contributions to waking empirical studies on peoples and nations from their theoretical slumber. Yet despite their originality and importance, their work has not led to significant progress in understanding the major questions at the heart of this field of investigation.

Intellectuals as National Actors

The correlation between work on "intellectuals" and on "nations" is not only due to the almost simultaneous development of these two fields. In these two domains, more than others, researchers were also more implicated in the object of their research. A person who studied the sociology of intellectuals was necessarily, by definition and profession, an intellectual. As a general rule, those who studied the history of intellectuals also wanted to play a role in the political debates of their time. Without necessarily signing petitions or joining a political party, some published articles in the press, gave radio and television interviews and took an active part in the "elaboration" of their society's political culture.

The same fascination syndrome can be found in the field of studies on the national question. Until the end of the 1970s, all those who helped write national histories were scholars with a well-established national consciousness. Observation of one's own collective history and national culture "from the outside" was almost impossible. For this reason, systematic appraisals of the subject were relatively rare. There were some exceptions, but you have to look at the intellectual biographies of Hans Kohn or Elie Kedourie, for example, to grasp the amount of distance necessary for the development of a slightly different awareness and the start of objectification of different research components.

There may be another reason for the surprising conceptual push in each of these fields in recent years. Minerva's owl only spreads its wings at dusk: the status of "intellectuals," like the position of "nations" in the West were so considerably shaken in the last quarter of the 20th century that it is impossible to think that there was no effect on the development of new thinking in these domains.

The shift in modern culture toward an era of audiovisual dominance has reduced the status of writers. From the revolution of printing in the 15th century until the middle of the 20th century, when television and film took on a larger role in the production and diffusion of knowledge and in shaping the collective imagination, the masters of the written word established a position of hegemony over the creation of high culture and, later, in the development of national mass cultures. In the third chapter of this book, we will see how much this position of control has been devalued by the rise of moving images. In mass communication, audiovisual producers and directors slowly but surely appropriated the power and prestige that journalists, writers, academics and teachers once enjoyed. While writing has not been completely eliminated, as the new symbiosis between words and images on the Internet has shown, and while intellectual writers are still thriving, it would not be too much of a stretch to say that their golden age is reaching its end. And this is probably one of the reasons that researchers can study them with a new analytical perspective.

The status of nations and their mass cultures have also undergone significant changes; however, the primary cause is not specifically related to audiovisual communication, although we cannot neglect its importance. Globalization of the production and distribution of moving images is still far from creating a uniform transnational culture, yet the power of its effects is reducing the autonomy of traditional national cultures and has led to the development of superstructures and sub networks of new and competing identities. Growing individualism has not weakened the need of human groups for self-determination, but the former hegemonic status of what I see as the heart of national consciousness, the close relationship between these collective definitions and higher political sovereignty, has started to erode. What people generally but imprecisely call "multiculturalism" is now on the rise in Western countries and is taking a new look at the forms and structures of national identity.

It seems obvious that the process of economic globalization and the displacement of the places where political decisions are taken are part of the slow but inevitable weakening of national sovereignty. The creation of the European Union and interventions by international organizations are only the tip of the iceberg of determinant morphological changes in the modern idea of sovereignty. It is still too early to tell what direction these changes will take, but we can say that the National State that developed over the past two hundred years will change in the 21st century.

Research on "intellectuals" and "nations" also seems to be a result of the infiltration of cultural history into the social sciences in the 1960s. Karl Marx once suggested that, contrary to common opinion, for which the past explains the present, it is generally the latest step that allows us to decode the previous ones. Reducing essential human activity in the West to the functioning of signs and symbols, the consolidation of consumer and leisure society, large-scale public cultural planning and communications in all of their forms have had repercussions on all human sciences. The cultural processes involved in forming kingdoms and States, in changing relationships of economic and social power or relationships between the sexes have taken precedence. Culture, cultural discourse and communications now occupy the place once reserved for labor and the economy as the modern "infrastructure" of historical development.

To a large extent, history and sociology have become "cultural," leading to the creation of countless cultural studies departments at the university level. And it is not surprising that the "authorized" agents of culture, intellectuals, have become legitimate and even privileged objects of research to increase our understanding of modern times. Focus on their contributions to politics, to the crystallization of norms and ideologies, and the interest in their cultural logomachies have produced abundant and constantly growing research.

Renewed investigation of the national phenomenon has also underlined the centrality of culture. While in the past attention was more often paid to long-term "ethnic" histories, to the formation of national market economies or state mechanisms of control that defined territorial and linguistic expansion, after the publication of Benedict Anderson's and Ernest Gellner's research, scholars started to look at the decisive role of culture in the relatively recent consolidation of nations. Benedict Anderson put the accent on "print capitalism" as the *sine qua non* condition for the start of the process that led to the creation of nations. The print industry, which allowed the easy distribution of books and newspapers, hastened the retreat of Latin and the suppression of local dialects, opening the way for the expansion of national languages that enveloped the new human entities. In parallel, Ernest Gellner offered the appealing hypothesis that the formation of a nation depends above all on transforming the codes of high culture into the common heritage of the whole society. While in pre-Modern, agrarian societies, the elite opposed the diffusion of written high culture, the world of accelerated industrialization, with the division of labor and the need for mobility, allowed for the creation of a homogenous mass culture.

These two pioneers brought an original perspective to the cultural strategies used to pass between national identity and politics, but curiously, they did not concentrate on the contributions of the agents of culture directly involved in these developments. The scholars who followed them have yet to fill in this gap systematically. Research dedicated to the Third World is an exception; in this domain, there have been advances in terms of the particular role played by intellectuals in the emergence of nations, their language and their culture.[7]

What was the status of the first intellectuals in Modern Europe at the birth of printing? Who were the primary agents charged with changing the administrative languages of pre-modern kingdoms into national vernacular languages? What relationships of power were established between the administrations of newly national States and the groups of intellectuals freed from the patronage on which they had depended? What did the new elite contribute to the widespread movement of nationalizing the masses that started in the last half of the 19th century? What responsibility did intellectuals—philosophers, writers, journalists and teachers—have in developing the conceptual content of the national imagination in different cultures? What is the connection between the position of historians in the field of ideological production and their generous contribution to shaping the dimensions of "long-term" national time? To what extent did the autonomy of intellectuals in liberal democracies contribute to the formation of a more overt national consciousness? How did intellectuals develop the idea of a "nation-contract" and how did they influence the masses that let themselves get caught up in the trap of an ethnocentric national identity? Did the universalist ideologies of "major" intellectuals serve sometimes as weapons used to defend national culture (like Marxism in France after the Second World War)?

The correspondences between the fields of research on "intellectuals" and "nations" and the response to these questions and many others could contribute to a better understanding of the secrets behind the invention of the nation and the ways in which its many different versions have spread around the world. They could also increase our knowledge of the various functions filled by intellectuals in different countries.

Simultaneous Creation

In this brief introduction and in the following chapters, I do not intend to respond to the historical and theoretical questions above. My aim is much more modest: for the past few years, I have been preoccupied with the question of the contribution of Jewish and Israeli intellectuals to the formation of the Zionist consciousness and the development of the Jewish-Israeli nation. I am also fascinated by the public and political status of different cultural agents in Israeli society. The history of Zionist intellectuals has not yet been the object of any serious study, no more than the characteristics of the Israeli intellectual field.[8] No modern society could exist without its intellectuals, when the concept is taken in its larger sociological sense as well as its reductive political meaning. It seems obvious that the Jewish national movement and Israeli society are no exception.

The first chapter of this book relates the initial characteristics of the history of Zionist and Israeli intellectuals. The following chapters attempt to fill in these broad strokes by analyzing some specific examples and specific time periods that will allow us to start understanding the connection between intellectuals and the Jewish national identity.

It is interesting to note that the terms "Zionist" and "intellectual" appeared at almost the same time and in the same place. "Zionism" had its hesitant beginnings at the start of the 1890s and gained more attention by taking a particular signification during the Dreyfus Affair. The same is true of the word "intellectual." It had already been used before the Affair but it became part of common language as a generic name as the Affair began to shake the public sphere. Is the simultaneity of the emergence of these two concepts a coincidence? Is there any correspondence between the two phenomena?

The popular summaries of the Dreyfus Affair sometimes give the impression of a single historical event that began in 1894 with the Captain's arrest for treason and ended in 1906 with his acquittal. This narrative follows the factual model of a complete story with a beginning, middle and end; it is a tragedy that has a happy ending. Yet wouldn't it be more appropriate to distinguish between two Dreyfus Affairs?

The first Affair starts with Captain Dreyfus' trial and the accompanying expressions of anti-Semitism, the events that are at the origin of the Zionist movement. The second Affair opens in 1898 with the publication of "J'accuse" by Émile Zola, when the image of the modern intellectual is born. A significant interval separates these two episodes, which allows us to have a better understanding of the emergence of Jews as a collective entity on the European political scene. And there is the first decisive appearance of intellectuals in the French public arena, also as a collective entity.

The lack of any intervention by intellectuals during Dreyfus' trial led to the publication of *The Jewish State* by Theodor Herzl,[9] then the convening of the First Zionist Congress in 1897. The identity discontent that had already started to grow a decade and a half earlier in the parties of the Yiddish people—who lived under the domination of the Russian and Austro-Hungarian Empires, and under a constant threat of pogroms and persecution—took a decisive step towards a Jewish national organization after the failure of the Enlightenment movement in the city of the "future" known as Paris. We could be sure that if "J'accuse" were published at the beginning of 1895 and not in January 1898, Zionism would have been born elsewhere and perhaps later. The deep pessimism and incisive perspicacity of Zionism's view of Europe's future, which grew rapidly in Eastern Europe, seemed to be confirmed in the intellectual political atmosphere in the Paris of 1895.

It is important to state that Herzl, a journalist from Vienna staying in the French capital, was not only present at Captain Dreyfus' military degradation ceremony. He had been a regular guest at the monthly meals held at the home of writer Alphonse Daudet and had met many prominent figures. Among them was Édouard Drumont, who made a strong impression on him.[10] During these encounters, Herzl became aware of something that optimistic liberals and socialists had a hard time admitting: scientific, aesthetic and spiritual progress does not necessarily come with moral progress; moreover, a deeper understanding of the world does not necessarily lead to greater tolerance for "alterity." Herzl could see the potential in the intellectual circles around Daudet and Drumont, the guest of honor. Unlike others, he did not underestimate their ability to read the mindset of the modern masses.

What caused the defeat of these intellectual circles of the Right three years later? I am not attempting to reexamine the reasons why the Dreyfusard camp emerged in 1898 or the factors behind its strength. Many scholars, from Christophe Charle to Jean-Denis Bredin have already studied those issues thoroughly with convincing arguments.[11] We should take note, however, that "intellectuals" appear on the scene after an event involving an officer of Jewish descent. This event not only had a major impact on the history of the Jews throughout Europe, but also contributed to clarifying the role of intellectuals as dominant agents in the development of components of the national imagination.

The constitution of nations, at almost each step of its stages in the 19th century and in the 20th, was marked by confrontations between those who supported an inclusive definition of citizenship ("jus soli") and those in favor of exclusive ethnocentrism ("jus sanguinis"). The formation of many different cultural systems in Nation-States came with battles between more universalist national approaches and holistic approaches based on an origin. It would not be justifiable to say that French, British and American nationalities were more political-cultural from the start or that German, Polish or Russian nationalities have always been ethno-biological or ethno-religious.

Yet the relationships of force between these trends were different depending on whether you look at Western Europe, North America or Central and Eastern Europe despite the fact that almost everywhere the specific character of a nation was the result of cultural combat. Intellectuals were not the only ones to weigh in on the ideological directions taken by the national consciousness. Social, political and economic issues as well as long-lasting mental characteristics have also forged the dynamic of the particular identity of each country.[12] Yet the weight of the written word and the ones who produce them—philosophers, writers, historians, journalists and teachers—was decisive in the development of the collective imagination.

The philosopher Johann Gottfried von Herder and the historian Heinrich von Treitschke were not the only source of ideological inspiration for the sizeable intelligentsia that laid the "volkist" foundations of the German nation. From Karl Wilhelm von Humboldt to Theodor Mommsen, several intellectual markers indicate the existence of a tradition more open to an accommodating for Germanity as it developed into a national culture. In the end, however, Mommsen and his peers lost out, despite their importance and influence, in the competition between collective identities struggling for hegemony in the Second Reich. Their failure joined a long series of elements that eventually led to the rise of National Socialism.

In the Troisième République, by contrast, Émile Zola and Anatole France took the advantage over Maurice Barrès and Paul Bourget. They relied on a long republican tradition and alliances with outliers in the Radical party who wanted to enter the government. Their victory was not definitive or unassailable. In the politics of defining national identities, the relationship to the Other, even a minimal Other remains an uncertain space: the French Jews arrested and deported in the summer of 1942 learned it the hard way.

Outside the interests of "power," the intellectual conflict that took place during the Dreyfus and Zola affairs had different conceptual levels: the universalism of justice, the relationship to Jews, disgust with moral corruption, the search for the truth, the army's role in the Republic, etc. Some of the leading Dreyfusards, according to their writings, were not free of prejudice towards Jews (Jean Jaurès among others). Contrary to what Émile Durkheim thought,[13] a particular sensibility to justice and truth is not always present in intellectual professions: the history of the 20th century has given us ample proof. The end of the cultural combat in 1898 depended on a series of specific historical circumstances that historians have already studied in great detail.

One of the most determinant circumstances was the fact that the solidity of the idea of nation, anchored in a civil and cultural tradition, served as a barrier to the rising tide of "ethnocentric" reflexes in France during the crises of 1890. Dreyfus was effectively denied membership in the French nation in 1895, but he was reintegrated in 1906. Zola, the object of public contempt from the "French" French because of his Italian origins, was admitted to the Pantheon in 1908.

A Jewish or a Zionist Imaginary?

We now know that young French writers of Jewish origin were particularly interested in the stormy period of the Dreyfus and Zola affairs.[14] But in all except one or two cases, none of them revealed a "hidden nationality"[15] at the time. Jewish intellectuals of Central and especially Eastern Europe became Zionists and a broad intelligentsia formed there to fill its ranks. What was the nature of the national imaginary that these agents of identity proposed to Jews from around the world?

A response to this important question can be found in the analyses of this essay. The development of the idea of a Jewish nation began long before the Zionist movement first started to take shape and continued long after the creation of the State of Israel. Isaak Markus Yost, the founder of Jewish historiography in the early 19th century, still described the Jewish past as the history of religious communities that emerged after the disappearance of the kingdoms of Israel and Juda. Only after the failure of the springtime of the people in 1848 did a new concept start to take hold and its main paradigms are still present today.

From historian Heinrich Graetz to philosopher Moses Hess, some intellectuals began to define themselves as members of a people-race that appeared two thousand years before the Christian era, was dispersed in "exile" in the 1st century of this era and was condemned to wander among other peoples. In fact, the dominant model for the reconstruction of a Jewish ethnic past showed similarities with the statements of the hegemonic discourse on the origins and long history of the German *Volk*. Pious British protestants had earlier started a movement that considered the Jews to be a foreign people that had to return to the Holy Land to be able to complete their conversion to Christianity, but it was in Germany that this idea found its "scientific" proof.

The model that made the Germans descendants of an ancient people-race was "borrowed" and applied to the "Jewish people of the East" born at the dawn of civilization. Historian Heinrich Graetz also took part in the debate between Treitschke and Mommsen on the question of whether Jews were part of the German nation and on the shape of the new nation, proposing a third dimension. The author of the vast fresco *Gedichte der Juden* (History of the Jews) expressed reserves about Treitschke and criticized him harshly, but in the end he adopted the analytical parameters used by the anti-Semite historian to define peoples and nations.

The oppressed took on the reverse image of the oppressor's judgment: where Treitschke held Jews in contempt, Graetz made them into examples of moral superiority rising above all others. Some Jewish-German intellectuals, feeling that they were being removed from the German cultural arena, took offense and decided to create their own national home. We should remember that they were only a small group on the margins; most writers "of the Mosaic faith" aspired to join Mommsen and participate in the *Bildung* of the German nation. They were absolutely convinced of their authentic Germanity, just like Swabians and Westphalians, and they were not wrong to think it because they were among the first Germans to take active part in transforming the codes of high culture into a national popular culture.[16]

The change started by a few isolated intellectuals during the 1860s and 1870s gained much more momentum at the end of the century. The intellectual and political camp around Theodor Herzl ascribed Jews with the status of a distinct "ethnic" nation and rejected the widely-held view that saw them as the descendants of dispersed religious communities. While Alphonse Daudet, Maurice Barrès and Charles Maurras mostly failed to integrate their ethnocentrist projects into French culture, they succeeded in saving important aspects of these projects on the "hard drive" of the memories of some of those that they were trying to chase away. Theodor Herzl himself was one of the least "volkist" among the Zionist leaders and intellectuals, most of whom saw themselves as the direct descendants of a Semitic-Jewish race that had no place in Europe.

In the 19th century, Ernest Renan already remarked that mistakes and forgetting were essential parts of forming a nation. The writing of most historians of peoples and nations has confirmed his remarks, and the agents of Zionist memory with their fertile memories are no exception. A prominent example can serve as illustration: because the existence of traditional Judaism was based on the belief of a metaphysical "exile" and religious aspiration for a sacred place, it was necessary for Jewish national agents to invent a historical discourse that implied the "exile of the Jewish people" following the destruction of the Temple in the 1st century of the Christian era to justify their secular "right to return" to the "homeland." It was hard to imagine, however, that a fundamentally agricultural people, not a sea-faring people like the Greeks or Phoenicians (or a people of merchants out for profit, as in the anti-Semitic imaginary) suddenly rose up and, without being forced to, dispersed so quickly.

Skillful historiographical acrobatics were needed to get around the fact that there were already more practicing Jews living outside the land of Judea than inside it well before the destruction of the Temple and that during this period the number of believers quadrupled, if not more (in an agrarian society that could hardly support so much demographic growth!). However, to suppose that Judaism was the first monotheistic religion to proselytize in the Greek world and the Roman Empire, to spread and develop until a large portion of the faithful decided to convert to Christianity—or to put it another way, to switch to more "user-friendly software" for reaching divine revelation—would have been heresy at the time when the nation was being formed. There was a need to produce an imperative narrative meta-discourse on an entire people uprooted by force, a people-race that began to wander around the world in search of asylum.

Renan's cold and lucid gaze on collective memory relied on his neo-liberal conception of the nation: he understood that a variety of possible choices existed in the modern invention of national groups. Like the Dreyfusards who came later, Renan finally (but not without ambiguity) opted for voluntary citizenship, which resonated with the dominant republican spirit after the country's defeat in 1870. Zionist intellectuals, for their part, preferred determining the shape of the Jewish nation with a common origin and blood ties instead of a "daily plebiscite." It therefore became impossible to join the persecuted nation and just as impossible to leave it. Unlike the Bund, for example, a movement that was active in Eastern Europe and developed an open and flexible national idea based on a rich and vibrant Yiddish culture, Zionist intellectuals addressed Jews around the world and because of the great differences in culture between the communities they had to trace the lines of national identity in biological and/or mythico-religious terms (see the second chapter for more on this subject).

This problematic image of identity gained strength and found stronger justification after the destruction of European Jews by the Nazis. For many, Zionism seemed to be right not only because of the accuracy of its prediction about the dangers of anti-Semitism but also because of its definition of Jews as a people "uprooted from its land" and needing to take root again as soon as possible. It was difficult to oppose the separatist Zionist arguments when Europe, with its political and cultural elite, had for the most part adopted the role of a passive witness during the massacre. Europeans then felt relieved to offer the Zionist enterprise land that did not belong to them.

The Jewish-ehtnocentric principle was confirmed with the expansion of colonization in Mandate Palestine, where it finally benefitted from a broad consensus as the basis for the definition of nationality in the State of Israel. Because of this "ethnic" principle, the Israeli Parliament, despite a secular majority, decided that only religious marriage would be recognized by law. Following this conception, it followed that strict, dissuasive religious conversion would represent the only way to join the Jewish nation (but not to leave it). As a result, until now, a significant portion of the land inside the borders of the State cannot be sold to a non-Jewish Israeli citizen. Since 1948, Israel has been recognized as the Jewish State even if a large number of its citizens are not considered to be Jewish and cannot join the "Jewish nation." They subsist as second-tier citizens, a sizeable minority that is unable to identify with the sovereignty that is supposed to represent them.

Since 1948, the majority of Israeli intellectuals persist in assuming the ethno-national image handed down by their predecessors. Writers, poets, filmmakers and journalists participated in shaping an original Hebrew Israeli culture that was totally different from religious culture but still chained to overall identity politics. They prefer to continue embracing an exclusive, holist State identity that only Jews can participate in, instead of working towards an alliance of all differences under a common republican identity.

In the past, some Israeli intellectuals spoke out against the foundation myth of an ancient and closed "ethnos." "Canaanite" writers in particular protested it before and immediately after the creation of the State. They tried to substitute another myth to secularize Jewish nationality to make it more civic-minded and open, but their influence remained limited. The first major cracks in the dominant conceptions of history and identity did not appear until the end of the 20th century.

The final chapter of this book deals with the questioning of these foundation myths to attempt putting them into their historical context. The press was quick to label this movement "post-Zionism." The phenomenon, which received wide-spread media coverage, caused the Israeli political and cultural establishment to break out in a cold sweat. The spirit of appeasement towards the Palestinian people, including recognition of the grave wrongs that they suffered and the republican principles defended by most of the actors in this movement led to hysterical reactions and blacklisting. The outbreak of the Second Intifada and the expansion of armed conflict "froze" the debate for a time and reestablished ideological "order."

All of the chapters of this book have already been published in Hebrew, and it can be read as the reflection of post-Zionist dissatisfaction with the characteristics of the dominant national memory in Israel. Its author, an Israeli Jew, believes that the best contribution to Hebrew society and culture in the Middle East includes both perpetuating the memory of the persecutions of Jews and an uncompromising confrontation of those aspects of the definition of identity the European persecutors were able to impose on the persecuted.

This painful confrontation requires the recognition of the "other people" and the expression of a desire for shared existence.

1

"People of the Book"

and People of Letters

> *It is sometimes surprising that something that once turned the world upside down now no longer disturbs it; the true people of letters are the reason for this phenomenon. Their minds are usually more independent than those of other men.*
> — Voltaire, *Dictionnaire philosophique,* 1757.

> *It is our misfortune that we are not a literary people but the people of the Book [...]. Yet the "people of the Book" has become a slave to the book, a people that has lost its soul and is lost in the written word.*
> — Ahad Haam, "*Torah of the Heart,*" 1904.

Tsahal, Claude Lanzmann's film dedicated to the Israeli army, closes with the image of a friendly young armor instructor at the helm of a giant tank. The officer, his face bright with intelligence, is wearing glasses with thin metal frames like those that are usually associated with intellectuals. The shot captures the film's visual hymn to the new Jewish warriors, hoping to show the audience that, although war is primarily the domain of soldiers, we can still see the intellectual heritage of the descendants of Marx, Freud and Einstein in the young officer's face. The powerful State of Israel has become the last refuge for an impossible universalism.

However, the first result of Zionist colonization was to change part of the "people of the Book" into a nation where, after many trials and tribulations, "people of letters" enjoy a position that is not very different from the one they have in other modern cultures.

The Birth of Zionism

A century before *Tsahal*, Theodor Herzl wrote *The Jewish State*. Like all of the other national movements of the modern era, Zionism first appeared in an exclusively intellectual environment, at the end of the 19th century. Theodor Herzl, who came up with the idea of Jewish political sovereignty, was a well-known journalist and an unsuccessful playwright. Max Nordau, his right-hand man, the "Trotsky" of the Zionist revolution, was one of the most popular and incisive cultural critics in Europe at the turn of the century.[1] The Bilu'im (a movement for emigration to Zion that was started in Russia after the 1881 pogroms and preceded political Zionism) consisted primarily of university and high school students. Until the First World War, young intellectuals filled the ranks of the Zionist movement. Only with the rise of Nazism and the creation of the State of Israel after the Second World War did the national Jewish movement begin to attract a more socially diverse population.

The fact that intellectuals were the first agents of national culture should not surprise us. In most national movements of the 19th and 20th centuries, people of letters were the principal ambassadors of modernity in the process of building collective identities. Because of the abstract nature of a national consciousness, a close-knit intellectual group was needed to ensure the organization and development of a new national culture. To borrow an idea from Ernest Gellner[2]—if forming a nation implies transforming the codes of high culture into a common heritage for an entire society, then the modern intellectual is without a doubt the cornerstone of the formation of any nation.[3]

The decline in the prestige of the rabbis, the traditional intellectuals of Jewish communities, was one of the decisive factors that contributed to the emergence of the "organic" (to borrow Gramsci's term), national and secular intellectual. A second important factor was, of course, the atmosphere of hostility and rejection that surrounded any intellectual of Jewish origin who left the cultural ghetto of his parents. Western national identities with greater self assurance led to assimilation, which was sometimes accompanied by a fear of the "other" and by eruptions of violent animosity. In Eastern Europe, the cradle of Zionism, open hostility towards Jews was almost always an essential cultural factor in the construction of new national identities.

This widespread hostility took many different forms: somewhat more civilized in the anti-Semitic expressions linked to linguistic heritage, and more violent in the riots and pogroms. Most of all, young Jewish intellectuals often faced exclusionary measures that denied them access to the new careers made possible by increasing divisions of labor. The discrimination was ratified into laws and decrees in the Russian Empire and the Kingdom of Romania; a more moderate form also existed in the German Empire.

New Jewish intellectuals who wanted to find a place for themselves in the ongoing process of socio-cultural modernization in Eastern Europe had three options:

1. Join the movement of massive emigration to the West, accepting integration into an unknown and completely foreign national culture along with the implicit risk of losing part of the symbolic capital they had accumulated until then—in other words, a loss of their social and intellectual status;

2. Participate, as intellectuals, in the activities of socialist parties, which—even though they used the codes of diverse national cultures—called for a universalism that erased the remnants of a specific identity. Socialist intellectuals of Jewish origin could thereby join a cultural and political camp with more familiar aims, one that allowed them to keep the advantages of their intellectual qualifications;

3. Create a new culture of their own based on traditional elements of identity that the process of modernization had started to dismantle—reconstructing and developing a specific culture distinct from both surrounding cultures and the pre-modern religious culture that had until then characterized Jewish communities. They would therefore be able to keep a higher status in their community, which maintained some of its characteristics despite changes and disintegration.

The third option quickly split into two main schools of thought. The first declared the possibility of creating a modern Jewish culture and ensuring its expansion without attaching it to the principle of an independent nation. The intellectuals who joined the Bund[4] and other autonomist schools along with them thought it was possible to conceive of and sustain a new autonomous culture without relying on the administrative apparatus of an independent State. The condition for realizing a project of this scale depended primarily but not exclusively on the advent of an internationalist socialist revolution.

Intellectuals in the Bund were therefore required to make certain compromises and include aspects of "lower" Yiddish popular culture to develop the values needed to ensure the participation of Yiddish-speaking craftsmen and laborers as equals in the hierarchy of the party. These characteristics helped give the movement its numeric strength and became the source of its vitality, but did not prevent its historic decline. Unfortunately, Lenin had a clearer perception than Vladimir Medem of the necessity of political power in concretizing national aspirations.[5] In the same way, Theodor Herzl's vision of the new link between sovereignty, power and national identity in modernity was more incisive than Otto Bauer's[6]—intuitively, if not in his theoretical statements.

The followers of the second current, who are the subject of this book, first occupied a marginal position. The participants from Central and Eastern Europe at the first international Zionist congress held in Basel in 1897 were intellectuals from a variety of professions and opposing ideological positions: students and journalists took their place alongside writers, teachers and doctors. Socialist high school students rubbed shoulders with unconventional rabbis and yeshiva (rabbinical school) graduates. There were also a few merchants, manufacturers and workers, but they were isolated elements.

The social history of the Zionist movement remains to be written, and it is difficult to give precise statistics on the socio-professional status of its first activists. Until now, the leaders and militants who rallied to this new national identity were grouped in terms of their political and ideological orientations. In Zionist historical syntheses, the intellectuals affiliated with the movement are generally presented as Jews without any particular social or professional status and are only distinguished by their specific national identity.

Yet it is hard to ignore the fact that the Zionist movement, perhaps even more than the Bolshevist party, essentially began as a minority intellectual movement without support from the masses. Zionism, a collective assimilation into modernity, was principally created by intellectuals who were often frustrated by the failure of their individual attempts to assimilate and by those who had made the deliberate choice to turn their traditional culture into a visible culture.[7]

The Zionist option represented one of the most difficult and radical options for a Jewish intellectual, even if it was spiritually one of the most attractive. For other peoples, the intellectual pioneers of their modernity were sometimes obliged to build a language, forge a collective memory, engage in political action or even serve in the army of the new nation. In addition to all of these tasks, young Jewish intellectuals turned Zionist militants had to leave their native country and, in most cases, break ties with part of their family to become expatriates in Palestine.

Despite the abstract fascination they might have with the country, its landscape, climate and indigenous population were completely foreign to them. And while many intellectuals were the architects (not the workers) of the process of transformation of peoples into nations, Jewish intellectuals also had to create, at least at first, a "people." Jews were not rushing to emigrate to Palestine. The lower middle classes occasionally expressed their sympathy for the national ideal, but the everyday struggle for survival was often too pressing for them. The peasant classes, who always formed a determinant majority in any people attempting to become a nation, were practically nonexistent in the socio-economic structure of Jews in Europe. For the most part, Jewish masses voted "with their feet," left for the West, turned to social-democratic parties, joined the Bund or chose to remain within their old religious and cultural orthodoxy.

Colonization is not an intellectual enterprise. The militant intellectuals of Zionism sought with all of their strength to create a new nation, and to this end some of them became professional politicians. Professional politics uses some of the same means of production as intellectual activity; and at the turn of the century, newspapers, brochures and books became tools for the politicians, just like the assemblies, committees, congresses or diplomatic meetings that made up most of the political-cultural production in the major European languages. By contrast, the intellectuals who decided to emigrate definitively to the new land that was to become a future homeland took the risk of facing radical changes in their social and cultural situation.

The Process of Colonization

Between 1904 and 1914, a wave of emigration known in Zionist historiography as the "Second *Aliyah*" (Second Ascent), laid the foundation for Jewish colonization in Palestine. In this particular case, historians have access to statistics that give an indication of the sociocultural stratification of the 35,000 immigrants during this period (some of whom returned to their country of origin or continued to wander farther to the west): 60% were between 15 and 30 years old and most were single; 23% held a baccalaureate degree without a profession, 15% held a university or higher education degree, and many had completed their studies in a yeshiva; approximately 50% spoke Hebrew more or less fluently.[8] There were apparently no illiterates in this group of young, educated immigrants, but the most fascinating thing that they brought with them was their ideological baggage.

While national identity in the 19th century was attached to the wave of democratic emergence that spread through Central and Western Europe, the national identity that appeared outside Europe in the following century emerged from a synthesis with socialist myths. In this context, the Zionist emigration movement was one of the first national movements in the 20th century to be built on the power of attraction of the promise of an egalitarian future. In contrast to the Zionist establishment in Europe, dominated by free-market ideology, many young candidates for emigration to Palestine defended the populist or socialist ideas that had spread through the Russian Empire before the 1905 revolution and in its immediate aftermath. Thanks to their belief in these egalitarian utopias, these sons of good families of the Jewish middle class could turn their back on the intellectual careers to which they were destined by their social milieu and become workers or farmers in their new land.

The "cult of work," the return to nature and collectivist socialism were seen as remedies to the social "anomaly" of Jewish life in Europe, and revolutionary romanticism was a convenient accompaniment to the needs of colonization. Aaron David Gordon, the prototype of the intellectual—a writer who became a farmer—was the cultural hero of this generation. Rejected by the intelligentsia and writers who lived by their pen, he contributed to the development of the ethos that called for an end to the division of labor between intellectual and manual activities.[9] Although most emigrants finally settled in villages, the young intellectuals who endeavored to conquer the land quickly gained an ideological hegemony and were the source of the generation of leaders who governed this society of new emigrants until the mid-1970s.

Among the emigrants who arrived in the two decades from 1904 to 1924, the years when Israeli society was formed, was David Green, later known as David Ben-Gurion, the founder of the State of Israel. There was also Joseph Haim Brenner, a brilliant but troubled Hebrew writer assassinated in 1921; Yitzhak Ben Zvi, the second president of the State of Israel; Shai Agnon, the future Nobel laureat in literature; Golda Meir, Prime Minister in the 1970s; and Haim Nahman Bialik, who was later considered the greatest poet of the new Hebraic culture.

The cultural needs of the small civil society that was starting to take shape led to a new division of labor between the political and the intellectual. Although the developing political establishment at the time actively participated in shaping elements of the national consciousness (and it was involved to a much greater extent than the political sphere usually is in already established societies), its administrative and organizational functions forced it to share the production of symbols for the new culture with a more professional group. The creation of a local center of political power was combined with the development of a community of cultural agents whose task was to supervise the production of elements of collective identity and memory.[10]

The relative autonomy from political power acquired by intellectual circles during the process of modernization in the West assumed a different form in a society of immigrants and colonists. This society, as we know, did not start with powerful and independent capital like a developed market economy; it did not have a large public of cultural consumers.

In addition, the continuing colonization efforts organized and administered by the political elite, directly related to the conquest of the land, gave them a prestige that was hard to challenge. Despite lacking the attributes of a sovereign State, the political establishment underwent a process of unification in the 1930s and through the political party and the unions, it succeeded in gaining a high degree of control over economic and social structures, in particular over the capital coming in as donations from abroad. This control also led to strict monitoring of the intellectual sector. The lack of independence of the cultural agents "authorized" by the pre-State political system was directly linked to the hegemonic ideology that would take hold of Israeli society starting in the mid-1930s.

The few attempts by intellectuals to establish their legitimacy by criticizing the political practices of the ruling class were doomed to failure. The "revolts" by isolated figures, like the great "extremist" poets Uri Zvi Grinberg on the right and Alexander Penn on the left, condemned them to be marginalized for years.[11] As we will see, only a handful of intellectuals were able to put up any lasting resistance.

The foundation of the "rebirth" of the language of the Bible in Palestine was built by Eliezer Ben-Yehuda, who could be considered the first "Hebrew" intellectual. He not only composed the first Hebrew dictionary, but he contributed greatly to the spread of this new language through his publishing work and his countless articles in the press. This does not mean, however, that Hebrew immediately became the dominant language of this society of immigrants in the early 20th century. At the time, few people spoke it fluently, despite the demands of national fashion. Modern Hebrew, or the "Israeli language," based on biblical Hebrew, Yiddish and completed with many neologisms, did not become the vernacular language of the Yishuv (the Zionist colony) until the 1920s.[12]

Joseph Haim Brenner, whose personality and literary activity marked an entire generation, could be considered the most prominent intellectual of this period. But it would be difficult to qualify the creative hub centered on a tiny publishing house and the sporadic publication of a periodical targeting a limited audience as a "literary field." It was only later, with the Bolshevik revolution in 1917 and the decline of Zionist activity in the major Jewish centers of Russia, that a distinct wave of "Hebrew" intellectuals arose. Most of them were forced to emigrate to Palestine (most leading Zionist intellectuals, however, emigrated to Central and Western Europe). The fact that this group only arrived in Palestine after the immigration of the pioneering youths who had come before the First World War contributed indirectly to consolidating the hegemony of socialist ideals in opposition to free market principles, and also to establishing very particular relationships between the political and intellectual spheres.

Officially, the Hebrew Writers Association (Agudat Hasofrim) was founded in 1921, but a Hebrew literary field was not truly formed in Palestine until 1924, with the arrival of Haim Nahman Bialik and his group and with the opening of the Dvir publishing house.[13] The Hebrew Writers Association, under the control of Bialik and in concert with the writers of the Zionist Left, became the necessary pathway for obtaining literary recognition, and the pages of its periodicals chronicle the stiff battles fought to gain notoriety. At the time, the Association saw itself as the spiritual avant-garde and the cultural guide of national revolution in the country.

Since many of the young emigrants from before the war were in fact the "spiritual offspring" of the emigrant writers from Odessa and Warsaw, they met their works with approval and respect, even if many of them were completely out of sync with their own social utopia.[14] The symbolic capital accumulated abroad by poets, writers and critics like Shaul Tchernikhovsky, Simha Ben Zion, Aaron Avraham Kabak, Yosef Klausner and even Bialik before their emigration gave them a privileged position to build an independent literary system when they arrived, and it also allowed them to keep the increasingly powerful political avant-garde from using literary production as a weapon for reaching clearly partisan political objectives. The conditions for its independence were that writers could not contest the growing political hegemony of the Zionist Left or interfere with its objectives.[15]

Most of the pioneering emigrants shared a veneration of books. However, the conquest of land and work (to make them "Hebrew" land and work) held the priority over the conquest of words and came before the development of Hebrew language, literature and education. An inevitable process followed, and the literary elite were finally brought to serve the political objectives of the new national homeland and its leaders. The 1930s were marked by a growing tendency to consider literature primarily as a tool for consolidating the ideology of the dominant party.[16] Even if it was understood that intellectual work should serve the cause of national renewal, a wide margin for maneuvering was tolerated at first. By the end of the decade, however, most of the leading members of the "Hebrew Republic of Letters" had formed a corps that could be mobilized along party lines and endeavored to produce literature with a social-national message.

The values of socialist Zionism became unavoidable and started to push literature that dealt with individual problems to the margins of the literary field and prevented debate over questions of form. The myth of the Hebrew worker, the pioneer farmer, the man or woman of action and not the producer of words fed the collective ethos in the 1940s, just as it fed the creative imagination. From the beginning, the Zionist enterprise was conceived to transform a hyper-intellectualized "exiled people" into a vigorous and productive nation: the process of giving form to this myth had started to reach its peak.

The original creators of Modern Hebrew poetry like Nathan Alterman or Avraham Shlonsky believed that they should join the ideological camp of movements on the Zionist Left and not hesitate to become active spokespersons. It must be noted, however, that the political parties were in a position to finance the publication of books and other publications and could therefore ensure stable literary production. More personal literature with a universal scope continued to appear; from time to time, intellectuals expressed doubts about the "immoral path" of concrete involvement in politics. But despite the occasional expression of disapproval, the heart of the literary system never produced any consistent intellectual critique of the practices of the political elite.

The relationship between the Zionist enterprise and the "non-Jewish Other"—even when it meant dismissal by Jewish bosses or expulsion from one's native land—did not elicit the disapproval or give rise to intellectual discussion in a literary milieu that, it must be noted, took the decisions of its national leaders for granted. The Arab population's violent opposition to colonization efforts starting in the early 1920s and especially in the major uprising and general strike in 1936[17] reinforced the Jewish society's "siege mentality." Local writers therefore abstained from any serious questioning that might harm the prestige of political leaders. It was practically impossible to integrate the new national community while publically questioning the pursuit of colonization.

The echoes of the Second World War heightened this politicization. The precarious existence of the producers of culture in a small, impoverished society in the throes of an acute economic crisis at the end of the 1930s made the assimilation of culture and politics even easier. Most writers were not in a position to live by their pen. The ones who did not write for the press worked as teachers, making them even more dependent on the political establishment.[18]

In the Opposition

Until the creation of the State in 1948, the Hebrew University of Jerusalem was the only intellectual organization capable of preserving a relatively high degree of autonomy. Founded in 1925, it became the privileged bastion of a surprising resistance to the power of political leaders, their systems of thought and their values. Most professors at the University brought a strong symbolic capital to Palestine like the writers who emigrated in the 1920s. They considered themselves to be the spiritual representatives of the Zionist movement as a whole, and not just servants of Hebrew society at the university. Their recognition in international academic circles and their personal relationships with the outside world encouraged their demands for cultural autonomy, which was a luxury in the 1930s. Most of the University's expenses were covered by direct donations, primarily from the United States, and the protection of its right to autonomy became a political challenge to the Zionist establishment.[19]

The most surprising opposition to the basic principles of colonization emerged from the lecture halls of the Hebrew University of Jerusalem. The Brith Shalom (Alliance for Peace) association, founded in the same year as the University, aimed to "reach a better understanding between Jews and Arabs."[20] It was an eminently intellectual association that had no intention of forming a political party. Akiva Ernest Simon, Georg Landauer, Gershom Scholem, Shmuel Hugo Bergman and the famous philosopher Martin Buber, who arrived in 1938, were members or participants in its publications. Judah L. Magnes, president of the University from 1925–1948, was connected to the group, and he often expressed its views. Many members of the University were not comfortable with these opinions, but they respected the status of those from the first generation of university scholars who tried to maintain the European liberal tradition in Palestine, despite the vicissitudes of colonization.

Yet the members of Brith Shalom were fervent Zionists, and many of them had taken leading roles in the movement abroad. Even though the main goal of Zionism was to establish a sovereign Jewish state, they were nonetheless defenders of a bi-national state. They concluded that Jewish demographic inferiority should be a factor of its integration into the region, and that continued immigration should be subject to Arab consent. Their views were, of course, totally rejected by the majority of Zionists.[21]

In fact, Brith Shalom and its successor, Ha-Ichud (The Union), were the most important organizations from the intellectual elite of the new Jewish society to oppose the direction taken by the process of colonization. The failure of these universal intellectual approaches and the start of the War in 1948 brought an end to the organized collective malaise caused by this opposition. Once the administrative machine of the new state was in place and the University became subject to the government's budgetary politics, protests against the process by scholars became more personal than collective (at least until the 1960s).

Brith Shalom was established and active in the marginal fringe of the Zionist Left at the same time that another group began to form in the margins of the Right and distinguish itself from the dominant Zionist consensus. During the 1940s, the literary milieu saw the appearance of a small group of intellectuals called the "Canaanites" in the history of Israeli society. Their territorial-cultural conception of the nation, offering an alternative to the ethnocentric national idea of hegemonic Zionism, was nonetheless formed in the heart of the Zionist Right.

Contrary to Brith Shalom, which was intimately linked to German culture, Canaanism took shape in Paris, and not by chance. The myth of the Hebrew nation that had turned the ancient Israeli period in the land of Canaan into an object of worship was inspired by French nationalist politics. Despite being in crisis, it still had a solid Jacobin foundation (perhaps influenced by the successes of fascist nationalism in Italy). The Canaanite movement represented a form of radical, pseudo-indigenous insurrection that tried to distinguish itself in the name of national pride from the religious discourse of past "exile," which it considered a subservient Judaism inherited from the oppression of the ghettos. According to intellectuals like Adia G. Horon and Yonathan Ratosh, settling in a new land should be founded on a solid, Hebraic culture that would unite the descendants of the Jews and the descendants of the Semites in the context of a return to a mythic Middle East.[22]

It is interesting to note that while many members of Brith Shalom came from an academic background, the Canaanites were mostly poets, writers, translators and artists. Their relatively small number and their position in the margins of the intellectual field should not be underestimated: this current had a significant influence on the newly developing Israeli culture, placing its stamp on several works and even, in some ways, on the Hebrew language itself. The insistence of its followers on an indigenous presence prefigured calls for a more authentic regional and local Israeli identity.

The Canaanites also had an important impact on political theory: they fed the thought of the radical Right, which called for the annexing of new territories after each armed conflict. However, the subsequent evolution of this cultural trend led to the most audacious positions on integration in the Middle Eastern sphere. Among the pioneers of reconciliation with the idea of Palestinian national rebirth after the creation of the state of Israel were literary critics such as Boaz Evron, Amos Kenan and Uri Avneri, whose intellectual roots drew on the ferment of ideas found in the literary circles of the Canaanite movement.

The Start of Sovereignty

The 1948 War,[23] the most difficult war fought by Israeli society, contributed to unifying intellectuals and the new sovereign power. Although the post-war era was marked by the publication of *Hirbeth Hizza* (The Ruin of Hizza), S. Yizhar's famous story of moral distress in the face of the expulsion of the Palestinians, who then became refugees, most cultural creation in the first decade of the new State's existence focused on celebrating national rebirth.[24] The intellectual classes quickly completed their integration into the new cultural establishment and contributed greatly to removing the boundaries between the State and civil society, which was needed for the quick consolidation of a new national culture.

As waves of immigrants arrived from Europe and Arab countries with less ideological motivation than their predecessors at the beginning of the century, Israeli intellectuals, personally motivated and with State support, developed an elitist Hebrew culture that disdained external contributions and aimed to eliminate any identity that was not strictly Hebraic. Already present before the creation of the State, this trend further reduced the contradiction in modern cultures between political power and an intellectual's thirst for independence. The responsibility given to the intellectuals to control the revolutionary cultural melting pot required total submission as well as the creation of a messianic cult of the State to replace the beliefs and traditions that the immigrants brought from their countries of origin.

Intellectuals, including survivors of the Holocaust and the ruins of post-war Europe, became a part of the process at a certain point—starting with a lesser role and suffering from the frustration of having to renounce part of their identity so quickly. Jewish intellectuals from the Arab world experienced even more difficulties at the beginning of the national revival: almost entirely excluded from official cultural discourse, they often suffered professional disintellectualization or were forced to emigrate to different countries.

Ben-Gurion, the charismatic first leader of the State of Israel, was never satisfied with political power alone; he also wanted to direct and shape cultural planning. His relationship with the intellectual milieu in the 1950s was particularly interesting and revealed the secret dreams of a self-educated man with a thirst for knowledge—he was denied access to higher education in Tsarist Russia—who may have wanted to become a "philosopher-king."

After combat had ended in the 1948 War, he gathered the most eminent Israeli intellectuals to develop "of a common accord" the cultural strategy that would guide the development of Israeli identity. Most intellectuals welcomed this flattering attention and did not hesitate to combine their cult of the State with a cult of personality.

Biblical study was the field of "research" that Ben-Gurion prized. He supported researchers but also engaged in original work on the subject himself. His intention was not to bring the "People of the Book" back to religion or tradition. His aim was purely national: to prove, using "ancient history," the Jews' right to ownership of the land (largely conquered in 1948 without compensation or reparations) and to strengthen the connection between the national consciousness and the new country's territory.

Transforming the precepts of the Bible into secular canons would also help the national memory bridge two troubling facts: on the one hand, some two thousand years of history of "dispersion in exile"—not a negligible period—during which the Jews were unable to develop the perception of a sufficiently national common destiny. On the other hand, the history of the "indigenous-temporary" inhabitants, more than 700,000 of whom fled or were chased out and forced to abandon their homes during the war. The unquestioned centrality of Bible study in the schools contributed in part to the subsequent development of Israeli territorial irredentism and reinforced the intellectual-official legitimacy of the latent fundamentalism that gnaws at secular Zionism in times of crisis.

During the first decade of the State of Israel, the writers of the generation of 1948, including Moshe Shamir, Aaron Meged, David Shaham and S. Yizhar—and the second generation of leading scholars at the Hebrew University, including the sociologist Shmuel N. Eisenstadt, the philosopher Nathan Rotenstreich, the historian Ben Zion Dinur, among many others, accepted the subordination of spiritual values to collective and state values as a historical imperative. Rational bureaucracy under an "enlightened" leader who was the object of unabashed intellectual admiration allowed Ben-Gurion, the first leader of the Israeli government, to establish a monolithic political culture, ignoring criticism from the Left and the Right.[25] In the 1960s, Shmuel N. Eisenstadt himself described the attitude of the cultural elite towards the State as "byzantine and sycophantic."[26]

Political-cultural relations were far from the model that was prevalent at the time in Eastern European countries. State authoritarianism never translated into a totalitarian approach and political plurality remained, along with the to and fro of constant conflict between different literary and artistic trends. It must be said that the dominant current of thought, which tended to limit as much as possible the expression of the deep conflicts underlying the cultural arena, never opposed intellectuals who organized committees and groups defending the Soviet Union—a common organizational practice in the 1950s that the international communist movement encouraged for reasons of manipulation.

In 1950, Israel saw the creation of a Peace Committee composed of public figures and intellectuals. The Committee housed representatives of the pro-Soviet Zionist Left and the Israeli Communist Party under the same roof. It had a brief period of expansion, but the growing tension between Israel and the Communist Bloc quickly cast these "fellow travelers" of communism into the margins. The small Communist Party then became the primary place of action for young Arab intellectuals who used its clubs and newspapers and their own impressive efforts to give limited autonomy, but rich in creative resources, to the local Palestinian culture.

Most Israeli intellectuals were docile in their acceptance of the cult of the State and in their veneration of its high priests, the army. The army was an effective tool in uniting masses of immigrants from diverse backgrounds around the government and the ruling party.

The 1956 War, during which Israel conquered the Sinai Peninsula in seven days, is a perfect example of political culture being swept aside by a wave of messianic militarism. Before the war, Nathan Alterman, the "bard" of the party in power, was asked to compose an ode to honor Hebrew arms. From the very start of the conflict, journalists described the war as a new revelation from Mount Sinai; buoyed by this atmosphere and following the victory, Ben-Gurion announced the advent of the "Third Kingdom of Israel."

Yet while the war revealed the hidden messianic current of the young Israeli culture, the conclusion of the conflict—with the complete retreat from the occupied zones of Sinai—reduced national tensions and redirected the new society towards a less "heroic" path of development. It marked the beginning of a process during which the influence of the State on different sectors of cultural production and diffusion was clearly diminished and intellectual enthusiasm for supporting this trend waned.

The years following the Sinai campaign saw a decrease in armed confrontations, a rapid increase in the standard of living and the first foundations of the Welfare State. Cultural and educational institutions were developed.[27] Tel Aviv University, established in the latter half of the 1950s, would become the leading university in the country. The number of students attending the two universities and the Technion (polytechnic school) in Haifa increased by 396% in ten years to reach 10,000 registered students.[28] The

"Republic of Letters" also underwent significant growth, welcoming a new generation of skeptical young creators known as the "State Generation." Readership of the independent press expanded, surpassing the official newspapers of the political parties. And David Ben-Gurion's stranglehold on power caused him to have many enemies, including in his own party.

In 1961, a grave political crisis, known as the "Lavon Affair,"[29] seriously divided the public sphere. The episode served as a miniature "Dreyfus Affair" for the Israeli intellectual world. The vast majority of those in the literary world who until then had rallied around Ben-Gurion's political power were quick to take the "philosopher-king" to task openly, criticizing everything that they had once admired in him. In January 1961, a number of professors from the Hebrew University signed a petition assailing Ben-Gurion as an authoritarian and antidemocratic leader and accusing him of using State institutions to increase his own power. Those in the government who opposed Ben-Gurion used this intellectual revolt and the accompanying atmosphere of protest to push the Prime Minister into retirement. The relationship between the cultural arena and the political sphere underwent a major change as a result of this crisis. For the first time, some sectors of intellectual production had the opportunity to extend their relative autonomy.

Towards the end of the 1950s, many producers of culture had already started to show the first signs of repugnance and refusal to take part in the development of a public ethos that required them to represent an idealized national collectivity. The new writers who appeared were too young in 1948 to experience the "miracle" of the "Kingdom of Israel's" rebirth. They considered the existence of the State to be a given. Poets and authors like Nathan Zach,

Amos Oz and A.B. Yehoshua began exploring literary domains where individuals were no longer sacrificed to society, or society to the State.

The Westernization of lifestyles in Israeli society at the time and the effects on the general mentality caused a change in the style of cultural production, with an accent on personal expression and more intimate individual experience. The previous generation of "founders" continued to dominate the centers of intellectual power, while nationalism and military heroism were still revered in schoolbooks and in the media. When Israel was opened to foreign investment, however, there was a simultaneous emergence of cultural models taking their inspiration from the West and the liberalization of modes of representation began to attract more interest.

The economic crisis of the mid-Sixties was a further impetus to the non-conformist modernist currents that saw the Israeli social experience as a starting point for creative thought rather than an object of veneration. The intellectuals who were politically active in these years engaged in a campaign of sustained protest to bring an end to the martial law imposed on the Arab population and to stop the process of expulsion from their remaining land. Martin Buber, the most eminent intellectual opposed to the "Ben-Gurion-style" culture of the 1950s, took a significant role in the protests organized against the government.

The Return to Colonization

The 1967 War[30] brought to a halt the slow process of "secularization" of the nascent Israeli nationality and the creation of a stronger "civil" culture. The tension that preceded the start of fighting and

the heady success of the Israeli army brought national messianism
back to the political center stage after a decline in the early 1960s.
The occupation of the old city of Jerusalem filled most "recognized" cultural agents with emotion and the cult of the newly
conquered land supplanted the former cult of the State. Unlike the
political elite in place whose surprise at the magnitude of the victory gave rise to questions and uncertainty, many organized
cultural producers and diffusers drank deeply from the elixir of
power and demanded the immediate annexation of all of the
"liberated" areas of the country.

Major intellectuals from across the political spectrum, including
the writers Shai Agnon, Haim Hazaz and Moshe Shamir, the poets
Uri Zvi Grinberg, Nathan Alterman and Haim Guri, and the literary
critics Dov Sadan and Avraham Kariv, called for the creation of a
Greater Israel Movement.[31] Other authors, teachers, journalists
and students followed in tow, each contributing in their respective
domain to the new annexationist plan. This effective political
action by intellectuals not only contributed to the rapid growth of
public opinion in favor of annexation but also pushed the government to return to the colonial politics of the "Promised Land."
Official geographers erased the Green Line (the border after the
1949 ceasefire) from old maps.

Yet there were no more young secular nationalists with no
chance of intellectual success in their country of birth, like the
immigrants at the beginning of the century, to legitimate the return
to colonization. The secular intellectuals of the Greater Israel
Movement did not go settle in the recently occupied land. A new
group of pioneers emerged: young non-Orthodox rabbis, graduates
of yeshivas or confessional schools, felt that their hour had come.
Up until then, they had lived in the margins of the cultural sectors

that held the high ground, and had even suffered from a certain anti-Judaism of the "Sabras" (people born in Israel). The modernization of Israel had relegated them to a subordinate position in the secular cultural arena.

Casting themselves as the "avant-garde" of national colonization, their status grew. Gush Emunim (the Block of the Faithful), composed of an alliance of politicians impatient to gain power and dynamic intellectuals—all veterans of the religious Zionist movement—undertook to conquer the land and carve out a position of relative hegemony for themselves within Israeli society.[32] Its successes in 1974 were surprising: the Zionist Left, in power since the creation of the State, found itself trapped by the myth of colonization and its own former slogan "One more dunam, (square kilometer) one more goat" and let itself be carried away by the movement, which led to the fall of the Left and the conquest of power by the Right in 1977.

Faced with the rising tide of nationalism after 1967, some intellectuals tried to moderate the blind enthusiasm of the Greater Israel Movement. The first to react and to react the most radically was the religious philosopher Yeshayahu Leibowitz, one of the editors of the Hebrew Encyclopedia. Just after the end of combat, he warned of the dangers of the June 1967 victory, which would transform Israel into a militaristic, oppressive nation and cause the complete loss of the Jewish spiritual tradition. Calling for an immediate withdrawal from the occupied territories, he was attacked and vilified; his voice remained solitary, like a prophet preaching in the desert. The culture of the far Left that had reached its climax in Western society at the time could not find a place on the Israeli political map, except in the creation of two small student groups on the margins of the Israeli Left.

While the Greater Israel Movement was born in the salons of poets, writers and journalists, the Movement for Peace and Security was conceived in university hallways.[33] Led by Yehoshua Arieli, with support from Yaacov Talmon, a celebrated colleague, and with the backing of writers and poets such as Amos Kenan, Amos Oz, Leah Goldberg and many others, this intellectual movement for peace attempted, without success, to counterbalance the political and intellectual Right.

The group opposed military messianism and called for a historic compromise to resolve the national conflict, using petitions and newspaper articles. It tried to convince the Israeli public that the Jewish settlement in Hebron was obsolete and it encouraged the first signs of appeasement from Egypt in the hopes of opening a dialog. However, despite the members' pledges of fidelity to the principles of Zionism and their support for accords that changed the border to ensure Israeli security, they were unable to use these positions to gather momentum for their movement. Their moralizing discourse, peppered with *Realpolitik* arguments, was unable to counteract the glorification of the armed forces and the temptation of territorial expansion. The intellectual elite that favored peace were unable to transfer its ideas to cultural agents or vectors of diffusion belonging to broader circles that saw territorial expansion as the true Zionist project. As journalists and communications professionals continued their habit of giving Hebrew names to the occupied territories, teachers showed no qualms at the erasure of the Green Line on official maps and happily took their students on field trips to the newly conquered territories of the "homeland." The Movement for Peace and Security disbanded after the 1973 War, unable to find a clear, unified position against the war's implications. The group's failure had both political and ideological repercussions. Consensus on national security gained the upper hand at a difficult time when the struggle for peace was in a state of emergency.

The 1973 War, a painful one for Israel due to the large number of victims, ended in a new military victory. Yet this victory was not as evident or as easy as its predecessors. These particular circumstances, combined with structural sociopolitical factors, helped weaken the government of the Left, the ruling party since the start of the nation, and led to its defeat by the Zionist Right. This political change was a major turning point in Israeli history and a particularly critical moment in the history of the relationships between the country's cultural elite.

From the 1930s to 1977, the uninterrupted domination of the Zionist Left was characterized by an almost total symbiosis between intellectuals and political leaders, punctuated, as we have seen, with momentary disputes and modest moral protests. The similarity in the social and cultural origins of these elites, the child prodigies of good families from the European middle classes, as well as the specific conditions of the new national society's formation, attenuated the conflicts that could have arisen from State control of the cultural arena. And by giving particular attention to this domain, official political discourse had always been able to come up with a priori universalist, socialist or liberal justifications of various national practices in order to reinforce the feeling of common affiliation between the political and intellectual elite. Menachem Begin's arrival in power thanks to massive votes from Oriental Jews and the support of religious nationalist sectors called into question this traditional symbiosis between a large portion of the intellectual classes and the direction of the State for the first time.

Unlike David Ben-Gurion, Menachem Begin, his great rival, had no concern for garnering the favor of the intellectual elite and did not seek their company. His target audience was different and his criticism of the cultural establishment contributed to his victory. His direct style, his nationalist-populist language and his obvious disdain for intellectual scruples heightened the antagonism from both leading intellectuals and the broader public of producers and diffusers of culture. Begin was the first Israeli leader to sign a peace accord with an Arab nation, but the average Israeli intellectual saw him as an anachronistic political leader who represented a superficial and inconsistent culture.

Many intellectuals therefore felt free to disagree with the government without hesitation and without the impression of betraying national interests. The idea, which they took no pains to hide, that the government represented "another people" was widely shared. The monolithic national culture that had strongly influenced Israeli politics until then continued to exist in the working classes, but started to retreat among the elite and was replaced by a pluralist and more open political culture.

The Likud government, the major party of the Israeli Right, having alienated the "high" intelligentsia, became less ideological and paradoxically more liberal; the autonomy of different domains of cultural production increased indirectly. At the same time, the prestige of these domains began to decline. From writers to professors, the public image of the intellectual started to lose the remaining symbolic capital that it had inherited from Jewish tradition, the very remains that had long been cultivated, preserved and instrumentalized by the Zionist Left.

The organization "Peace Now" was formed in this context at the end of the 1970s. Like many other similar organizations, this pacifist protest movement came from typical intellectual circles. Unlike its predecessors, it was able to establish a relatively large base and rally sizable numbers during major public protests. The peace agreement with Egypt helped strengthen the movement even more by attenuating Israel's long-standing siege mentality.

The start of the 1982 Lebanon War[34] did not weaken the movement; on the contrary, it increased its intensity. After the Sinai campaign in 1956, it was the second war that Israel started of its own initiative. Yet while the Sinai campaign met with almost universal support, the Lebanon War, the first war under the leadership of the Right, met with immediate disapproval and intellectuals began to criticize it even before the fighting ended. The denunciation of an ongoing war was an entirely new phenomenon in Israel and marked the beginning of a new era.

The world of intellectual production responded in unison. First, during a brief period, a vigorous and widespread artistic opposition took the lead, primarily in the production of highly politicized works: novels, plays and poems began to treat subjects of a political nature with critical distance. In structures dominated by the official ideology, such as schools and the State-controlled media, the changes were not immediately apparent. In universities, however, where professors spent part of their time in training abroad, in the networks of the privately-held press and particularly in local newspapers, new political sensibilities began to take shape.

As respected authors such as S. Yizhar, A.B. Yehoshua and Amos Oz continued to support the Labor Party's return to the place that had been "stolen" from it at the head of the government (with the hope of restoring the status that had been taken from writers by the same token), another intellectual sector, cinema, began to create surprising and unconventional images. The most significant change in the organization of the cultural field took place in the film industry. This sphere of cultural production, the least encumbered by the weight of the written word, became a place of amazing innovation. It was as if the Hebrew language had been an effective barrier against the revelations of a few collective memories that continued to lead a disturbing existence in the unconscious. Unlike writers, the directors' mastery of images was less dominated by the proven codes of a language created by the cultural founding fathers.

Despite the inherent standardization of the conditions of cinematographic production, the 1980s saw a number of films directed by Israelis, like *Hamsin*, by Daniel Waxman; *Beyond the Walls*, by Uri Barbash; *Fellow Travellers*, by Yehuda Ne'eman; *On a Narrow Bridge*, by Nissim Dayan; *The Smile of the Lamb*, by Shimon Dotan; and *Esther*, by Amos Gitai.[35] These works were not anti-Zionist; some of them were even marked by a feeling of Jewish national superiority. But in one way or another, they all presented Israeli reality in a situation of conflict with an "Other" that, due to circumstances, was unable to lead a normal life. The repressed of the Zionist unconscious reappeared in the national consciousness, contributing largely to changes in the definition of the collective "I." The young film industry sometimes appeared to presage the future Palestinian Intifada, which broke out in late 1987.

This "Palestinian" wave of Israeli films soon faded, but the first Intifada, which led to the Oslo Accords,[36] paved the way for new relationships of force in the intellectual domain.

From One Intifada to Another

For almost twenty years, the majority of Israeli intellectuals denied that the nature of Israel's presence in the territories was fundamentally colonialist. Most adopted terminology that described the territories as "administered" instead of "occupied" and those who recognized the state of occupation referred to it as a "liberal occupation."[37] The Palestinian popular uprising in December 1987 ended this illusion and the centrality of national conflict became one of the highest priorities of engaged intellectuals in Israel.

A few weeks after the first violent protests in Gaza and the West Bank, groups of students from the Literature and Social Sciences departments of Tel Aviv University began to organize committees to protest the use of real bullets during the repression of the protesters. Six hundred members of the university signed a petition against the occupation and for an Israeli peace initiative. At the same time, two hundred and twenty celebrated painters, sculptors and photographers exposed their work in seven Tel Aviv art galleries in protest against the repression. The traditional barriers between the majority of intellectuals on the Zionist Left and the non-Zionist minority seemed to be on the point of definitively disappearing. As in the final phases of the 1982 Lebanon War, a broad front of intellectuals appeared on the public scene, unified by the refusal to accept the policies of a government under the direction of the Right, which was stuck in its negation of the existence of a Palestinian national entity.[38]

It must be noted that during the first two years of the "Stone Intifada," 586 Palestinians were killed in the territories, including 37 children under the age of 12 and 94 between the ages of 13 to 16. On the Israeli side, there were 19 victims, 10 soldiers and 9 civilians, including three young girls. The "balance" of the blood spilled was cruel and tragic but the result remained "relatively acceptable" for the Israeli intellectual Left, which began to receive support from a growing periphery. In December 1988, the Peace Now movement succeeded in organizing a large protest under the banner of opening talks with the PLO. One year later, Peace Now organized the first major meeting with representatives of Palestinian organizations in Jerusalem. Renowned writers and academics expressed their support for the need to begin talks by means of articles in the press. For the first time, the main publishing houses published research that called into question the official history of Zionism and the creation of the State of Israel. The concept of "post-Zionism" attributed to a new generation of young intellectuals—researchers, essayists and even poets—made its way through various circles and received support from some university students. (Given the importance of this movement in Israeli intellectual history, the last chapter of this book will be dedicated to it.)

Public turmoil and contestation did not stop Israeli authorities from sequestering Palestinian universities for an indefinite period. During the uprising, these small universities served as bases for organizing mass demonstrations and building roadblocks in the West Bank. Israeli university associations did not express the slightest solidarity with their Palestinian colleagues, no more than student unions or the Hebrew Writers' Association. Each justified its inaction by stating that they did not get involved in politics and only took action on issues related to their profession.

The limits and the weakness of actions by intellectuals, the defenders of peace, in the face of the Palestinian insurrection were later confirmed by their positions during the conflict between Iraq and the United States and Western countries after Iraq's occupation of Kuwait in the summer of 1990. Many Palestinians expressed their support for Saddam Hussein, while the vast majority of Israeli intellectuals condemned these manifestations of sympathy and, from the start of the hostilities in January 1991, expressed their enthusiastic support for the Western coalition led by the United States. The thirty-nine Scud missiles that fell on coastal cities in Israel and the joy shown by many Palestinians for this "Arab" show of force reactivated the "victim syndrome" in media broadcasts and other vectors of Hebrew cultural production (for more on this subject, see Chapter 3). The tenuous relationships established between Israeli and Palestinian intellectuals did not survive the experience. The increasing violence of the Intifada and its extension in the form of deadly attacks in the occupied territories and inside Israel did little to encourage continuing the opposition that had begun in the late 1980s.

However, while Palestinian violence repelled the most eminent Israeli intellectuals and quieted the few expressions of sympathy for the struggle in the territories, it created a growing lassitude among "ordinary" Israelis. The Scuds fired from a distant country gave the lie to the traditional idea that control of the territories gave the State of Israel a security perimeter that was essential to its survival. Moreover, this "protective perimeter" was becoming the crux of the problem. The public's new awareness also contributed to the close victory of the Left under the leadership of the Labor Party. In June 1992, Yitzhak Rabin, the Chief of Staff of the army during the 1967 War, formed a government with a parliamentary minority that seemed to put Israel on a new path.

The role of the cultural elite in the electoral victory of 1992 is hard to measure. It is clear that a majority of secular writers supported parties on the Left, although this support lacked the conviction for mobilization; on this occasion, the increasing erosion of their prestige became clear. The retreat of grand ideologies among the Western intellectual elite had reached large sectors of Israeli culture. However, even if intellectual contribution to change in the political climate was relatively limited, the victory of the Left block opened up new possibilities for public action and hierarchic promotion.

In building his government, Rabin was not bold enough to name a minister from the Palestinian-Israeli community, but he called Shulamit Aloni, a leader of the left wing of the Labor Party, to serve as Minister of Education and Culture. Trained as a lawyer and a former Bible Studies professor, Shulamit Aloni energetically supported intellectual projects that had been sidelined by the previous governments on the Right. As Minister of Education and Culture, and later as Minister of Communication, Science and Art, she worked to improve the image of intellectuals—writers, researchers and university professors—and was even behind the initiative to award the prestigious Israeli Prize to Yeshayahu Leibowitz. As noted above, this famous orthodox religious philosopher maintained a vigorous denunciation of the occupation and called for the immediate withdrawal from all of the territories until his death in 1994. In the year when his candidacy for the award was announced, he went as far as saying that "religious nationalism is to religion what National Socialism is to socialism."[39] His words led to a public outcry and a wave of opposition to his nomination for the prize. After Rabin declared that he would not participate in the awards ceremony, Leibowitz rejected the official honor and his candidacy was removed.

In the same year, Rabin had the Israeli government sign the Oslo Accords with the PLO. For many reasons, this event represented a break in the Israeli national consciousness. The Israeli government's consent to recognizing the representative organization of a Palestinian national entity and to begin a first withdrawal of armed forces from some of the occupied cities elicited both support and hope from the community of secular intellectuals in the Zionist Left, while causing a profound shock to the colonists and the orthodox religious intelligentsia that supported them.

While numbers and institutions favored the intellectual Left, ideologically, its weaknesses came to the surface.

A clear drop in ideological tension affected all of the intellectual fields of the Left, while the Right preserved its mobilizing energy. National-religious intellectuals had dedicated themselves to sanctifying the "Land of Israel" after the 1967 War: they spent the majority of their educational and propaganda efforts on changing the religious precepts of Judaism into a patriotic-territorial faith while preserving an envelope of ceremony and clerical rhetoric and giving it a modern form. Translated into effective action, these efforts were rewarded and the number of colonists in the territories on the eve of the Oslo Accords had reached almost 100,000. The corrosive effects of this success on the orthodox religious public caused leading rabbis to adopt the terms of territorial modernity and use them in their sermons.

The most recognized left-wing intellectuals—the writers Amos Oz and A.B. Yehoshua, philosophy professors Shlomo Avineri and Yirmiyahu Yovel, reputed literary critics Menahem Brinker and Gershon Shaked, to cite only the most prominent ones—all agreed on the need for a rapid withdrawal from the "administrated" territories. Their call for withdrawal was based more on the immorality and ineffectiveness of the oppression of the "other" than from the conviction that these territories were not part of the legitimate heritage of the Jewish nation. Against the "strong" argument of the "unique and indivisible" nature of the historical homeland, the Left only raised a tentative argument that shared important points with the basic positions of the colonizing Right.

When the government began to transfer control of part of the territories the Palestinian Authority under the leadership of Yitzhak Rabin and Shimon Peres, this political action did not lead weary left-wing intellectuals to engage in any fresh thinking or profound work to change the public's mindset. Rabin began the process of "dismantling" the Jewish "homeland" without any prior intellectual preparation of the Israeli public. He paid for it with his life.[40]

Yigal Amir, the government leader's assassin, was a law student at Bar-Ilan University. This university, closely tied to the national-religious party and a jealous defender of its religious status despite receiving State funds, was one of the primary institutional centers for training of national-religious intellectuals, along with the high rabbinical schools (the yeshivas). The university's leaders were quick to condemn the crime and had to dismiss a teacher in the history department who made derogatory comments about the late Yitzhak Rabin; however, opposition to the Oslo Accords among its professors of religion (approximately one-third of the teaching body) was vigorous and determined. Marches by Bar-Ilan students against the peace accords were much more rowdy than on other campuses. Bar-Ilan University also encouraged and took under its patronage the first academic institution created in the occupied territories: the College of Judea & Samaria. Founded in 1982 in the Ariel settlement, its priority was obviously to accept Israeli students and the inhabitants of the territories around it. The college is still in operation today under the auspices of Bar-Ilan University, and the government has even proposed to make it an independent university.

For the sake of objectivity, it must be noted that Bar-Ilan not only housed the reputed literary critic Hillel Weiss, one of the most virulent ideologues of colonization, but also Menahem Klein, a pacifist and religious orientalist, who was able to teach there despite the ambient nationalism.[41] He represented a minority within the minority in the university bastion of clerical nationalism, but his presence on the teaching staff allowed the university to maintain a pretense of liberalism.

The colonizing Right spread its ideas primarily through rabbinical schools, and as noted above, through the sermons of the organic intellectuals of religious nationalism: the new, militant rabbis. The right-wing cultural elite also ran a radio station, several publications, like the newspaper *Nekuda* (*Point*) and *Nativ* (*Road*), as well as a number of websites. *Nativ* was supported by an organization of intellectuals in the full sense of the term: Professors for a Strong Israel. The official condition for entering the circle, founded in 1988, was to hold a doctorate degree. During the Oslo Accord negotiations, its activities grew and drew more attention from the media. Its declared objectives were protecting the land of Greater Israel, preserving the "Jewish character" of the State of Israel by any means necessary, fighting post-Zionism and adopting free-market economic principles. Its members came mostly from among researchers in the natural and exact sciences. Its leading figure was without question the economist Israel (Robert) Aumann, Nobel Prize laureate in economy in 2005.

In parallel to these diverse intellectual currents of the religious Right, the Shalem Center was founded in Jerusalem in 1994 as a new, dynamic center that did not attract much attention when it began. Its founder was Yoram Hazoni, an energetic, emigrant intellectual from the United States, where he had published essays on Israel and Zionism.[42] A noted representative of the new Right, he soon began publishing a general interest journal, *Techelet* (*Azure*), and engaged in national politics by becoming a close advisor to Benjamin Netanyahu, one of the leaders of the Likud. The activities of the Shalem Center were funded by the American cosmetics magnate Ron Lauder. His liberally dispersed funding allowed the organization to establish generous grants, fund archaeological digs and start a publishing house. During the 1990s, the center became a pole for various intellectuals who were concerned about the perspectives of peace and the effects of a society of affluence on the country.

The success of this private institution was not only the result of its financial security but also of the almost total collapse of the Zionist-socialist hegemony over the Israeli intelligentsia. The rapid privatization of the economy, the waves of emigration from the former Soviet Bloc that were hostile to any return to state collectivism, and the success of Israeli high technology contributed to the formation of a political and intellectual camp that was both neoliberal in its economics and nationalist in its politics. The emergence of a similar Right in the United States gave added weight to the local ideologies.

The arrival of more than 1 million emigrants in Israel after the fall of the Soviet Union gave rise to an effervescent emigrant intelligentsia that continued to create and express itself in Russian, its mother tongue, and showed no hesitation in expressing its disdain for "indigenous" creation in Hebrew. The economic and institutional difficulties this intelligentsia experienced in integrating did not allow it to bloom fully and make use of all of its symbolic capital; its members preferred to stay behind the walls of a cultural and linguistic ghetto rather than integrate the local culture. During the 1990s, their antagonism with Hebrew producers of culture seemed to cause more harm to their creative forces than the national conflict itself.[43] However, a deep hostility towards the Left and feelings of Eurocentric superiority towards the Middle East were common among immigrants from the former Soviet Bloc, and many joined the ranks of Right-wing Israeli political parties.

Israeli intellectuals adapted to multiculturalism as its legitimacy grew: by the 1990s, Israeli culture had developed a sufficiently solid base to feel no threat from a multiplicity of languages and traditions or from revealing some of its own lines of development. The idea of a unidimensional nation was on the decline in most of the Western world in favor of a pluralist and relatively more tolerant identity politics. The major intellectual trends adopted in Israel often came from the United States, and American enthusiasm for pluriculturalism was followed by many members of the Israeli intelligentsia.

This new climate also favored the emergence of a group of Mizrahi intellectuals. The 1980s had already witnessed the success of a political party, Shas, which had its origins in Mizrahi religious orthodoxy. Its founders were in revolt against their spiritual leaders and had studied in rabbinical schools of the Ashkenazi tradition (Central Europe). In 1996, a current composed of secular intellectuals of Mizrahi descent also appeared on the public stage. The Mizrahi Democratic Rainbow Coalition consisted of young professors, of which the most famous was Yehouda Shenhav,[44] educators, teachers and filmmakers. What was interesting was that most of them were Left-leaning and some of them even defined themselves as non-Zionist. The group refused to organize itself into a political party even though its production was not limited to purely ideological and cultural endeavors. Its political and legal struggles led to jurisdiction in favor of public housing primarily for Israeli citizens originally from Arab countries, who were mostly concentrated at the bottom of the social ladder.

Despite its initial success, the number of members of the Mizrahi Democratic Rainbow Coalition remained limited. Its critique of the Eurocentrism and discrimination suffered by immigrants from Muslim nations at the hands of the institutions of the Zionist establishment on their arrival in Israel touched a major cord. Yet the pluricultural project that it submitted to Israeli society contained a major sticking point. While Mizrahi folklore had grown in popularity since the 1970s and especially since the Right's rise to power in 1977, it was still necessary for it to appear unconnected to any Arab culture. The desire to dissociate themselves from their Arab origins to integrate as much as possible in the Zionist enterprise was the lot of the majority of Jews who came from primarily Muslim countries. To integrate, they valorized the distinctive religious signs of their identity that comforted them in their Judaism and downplayed the elements of secular culture brought from their native lands as much as possible. (From this perspective, Zionism, essentially a secular movement, hindered the secularization of these immigrants.)

The intellectuals of the Mizrahi Democratic Rainbow Coalition and some of their predecessors, like the talented writers Shimon Balas and Sami Michael, demanded recognition of the dominant secular cultural specificity of immigrants from North Africa and the Middle East—in other words, legitimizing the expression of the secular Arab components of their original culture. This aspect did not receive the support sought for it in the community, which also explains why the graduates of rabbinical schools were able to form an orthodox religious party (Shas) by recruiting voters from the Mizrahi Jewish sector.

Shas, which at first did not appear to be a right-wing party, turned to the Right at the end of the 1990s. In the end, maintaining the prerogatives of Judaism in a Zionist State won out over promoting the diverse cultural origins of the immigrant generation. The Right's return to power under Benjamin Netanyahu in 1996, with support from Shas, put a new hold on the Oslo peace process, which was experiencing difficulties after Rabin's assassination. During the years of the "Oslo Peace," colonizing settlements in the occupied territories increased, especially from 1995 to 1999, when the number of colonists doubled to reach 200,000. Other than this "demographic success" that the right-wing coalition claimed as its own, Benjamin Netanyahu's new government failed in almost every other domain, and paved the way for the Left's return to power three years later. Ehud Barak became the leader of the new left-wing coalition, and secular intellectuals could once again dream of a bright future.

From Intifada to Disengagement[45]

Like Yitzhak Rabin before him, Ehud Barak had been Army Chief of Staff and his military prestige played no small role in the Left's return to power. Ehud Barak's relationship with intellectuals was not particularly warm, but he found it useful to call on the services of two renowned intellectuals of the Zionist Left in his government: Shlomo Ben Ami and Yuli Tamir. Shlomo Ben Ami, a historian teaching at Tel Aviv University, had already served as Israel's ambassador to Spain under different governments on the Right but had never cut his ties with the Labor party. Yuli Tamir taught philosophy at Tel Aviv University as well and was one of the founding members of the Peace Now movement. Shlomo Ben Ami was named Minister of Internal Security (and therefore of the Police) and Yuli Tamir was named Minister of Immigrant Absorption. By handing them these dossiers, Barak showed his relatively clear disdain for intellectuals who aspired to be politicians. He showed the same disdain for the Arab voters who had supported him en masse as well as for his interlocutors in the diplomatic negotiations that took place over the two years of his term.

Like his predecessor Rabin, and despite the fact that 95% of the Arab population of Israel voted for him, Barak did not name a single Palestinian-Israeli minister. His neglect did not trouble left-wing intellectuals, including the two named to the government. Progress in the peace process was more important to them at that stage than improving internal relations between the Jewish and Arab communities.

However, the continued exclusion of the Arab electorate from the centers of political power, as well as from economic and intellectual power, heightened the feeling of alienation of the Palestinian-Israeli generations that were born and educated after 1948. These young intellectuals displayed more audacity and independence than their parents, who had witnessed the "national disaster" of the creation of Israel. In the eyes of the youth, the first Intifada also had the effect of valorizing their Palestinian identity and transforming their political and cultural relationship with the inhabitants of the occupied territories.

While the writer and essayist Anton Shammas could still recognize the hegemony of Hebrew culture in the mid 1980s and at the same time call for Israel to be the "State of all Israelis" and not the State of all Jews in the world,[46] in the early 1990s this approach was obsolete in the eyes of the young intelligentsia and was replaced by the demand for a "State of all its citizens" without a specific identity determined from on high. The expression became the slogan of some Palestinian intellectuals in Israel whose political spokesperson was Azmi Bishara.

The personal story of this political philosopher is emblematic of the situation of Arab intellectuals in Israel. We have already seen how the Arab intelligentsia of the country found refuge and protection in the small Israeli communist party after being completely rejected by cultural circles. The party used its ties with countries in the Soviet Block to send its most promising youths to pursue higher education in Eastern Europe. It ensured the education of its future leaders and contributed to the emergence of an intellectual elite. Yet while medical students had some chance of entering the Israeli marketplace at the end of their studies, graduates with literature or social sciences degrees faced insurmountable obstacles. Azmi Bishara came back from East Berlin with a doctorate in philosophy and like many of his peers he found no university doors opened for him, despite his talent. While Anton Shammas lost all hope and decided to move to the United States where he was offered a post at the University of Michigan, Azmi Bishara left behind intellectual work to enter politics, like Shlomo Ben Ami and Yuli Tamir. Along with a few other young intellectuals, he created an Arab opposition party. He was elected to the Israeli parliament and presented his candidacy for Prime Minister in a gesture of unrealistic protest.[47]

This new stroke of Arab "bravado" raised more than one eyebrow in Israeli intellectual circles. Ehud Barak was a popular figure there, linked to an image of an authentic representative of the peace camp. When he started negotiations with the Syrians at the end of 1999, it seemed that he would answer all of the hopes placed in him. The writer Amos Oz, the most respected intellectual on the Left in the late 1990s, immediately offered his support, while offering the following advice: make peace, but not at any price. Amos Kenan, another of the well-known authors favoring peace, signed a petition calling on Ehud Barak to enter into negotiations but to sign an accord only if the Israeli settlements in the Golan Heights remained intact. Myron Benbenisti, one of the leading essayists in the same camp insisted that there should be no falling back to the old border from before 1967.[48] Listening to general public opinion rather than the recommendations of these three intellectuals, Ehud Barak did not renounce some of the 1967 gains and negotiations failed.

In 2000, Ehud Barak hoped to conclude accords with the Palestinians quickly despite the fact that he had avoided all negotiations with the Palestinian Authority since taking power. The historic meeting in Camp David under the patronage of Bill Clinton also ended in total failure. During these talks, the Israelis categorically rejected, once again, the solution of the 1967 borders as a basis for resolving the conflict, while demanding that the Palestinians declare themselves ready to recognize the historic end of the conflict. For the Israeli public, Yasser Arafat was fully responsible for the failure of the talks and the outbreak of the Al-Aqsa Intifada after this setback was considered by most circles, on the Left and on the Right, as being a well-orchestrated plan by the President of the Palestinian Authority.

Why did intellectuals on the Left as a whole accept the positions of the Barak government without debate despite their growing support for Palestinian national claims since the First Intifada? The answer to this question contains the key to understanding the particular position of the intellectual in the modern cultural domain and for solving the ideological code that had dominated Israeli intellectual circles since 1967.

Intellectuals engaged in politics, be they writers, researchers or university professors, use print and electronic media to get daily information on the political situation like most citizens. Since the 19th century, they have been distinguished, however, by their intellectual gifts, their ability to cast a critical eye on the flow of information from the press. But in the face of the power of moving images, which have increasingly become the model for political representation in the last quarter of the 20th century, intellectuals of the written word have found themselves in a position of relative inferiority. They were not trained to decode visual vocabularies systematically in their organic connection to the general framework of transmitting information on screen. (I will come back later in this book to this aspect of the cultural domain.)

When broadcasting the first news on the progress of the talks at Camp David, the audiovisual media projected an almost idyllic image of the Israeli government leader, an experienced orator from the political Left who was ready to go far in his diplomatic proposals. The fact that he brought the historian Shlomo Ben Ami with him to participate in the negotiations increased the intellectual respectability of the Israeli team, as opposed to their opposite numbers represented by Yasser Arafat, a "problematic" figure. The Palestinian leader had never been very comfortable speaking English, never understood fully the cultural codes of the West and obviously had no ease in reaching the Israeli public through the media.

Coverage of the Camp David summit on the leading Israeli television channel was orchestrated by Ehud Yaari, a talented orientalist journalist who had been elevated to the role of national commentator on the entire Palestinian strategy.[49] Yaari had already developed a dislike for Arafat during the period of the Oslo Accords. From the start of the Camp David negotiations, he began a campaign of systematic disparagement of the Palestinian leader. Most other, less qualified commentators followed his lead and together they succeeded in creating a critical symbiosis against Arafat using convincing representations and terminology. The average Israeli intellectual does not understand Arabic; the internal discussions of Palestinian society are foreign to him or her.

Confronted with the "important concessions" made by Ehud Barak, according to the daily reports of the Israeli media, he or she was taken in by the fascinating logic of the little screen. Amos Oz exposed this peculiar situation clearly in his introduction to an important article published in the *New York Times*: "I am sitting in front of my television, in my living room, and I see Yasser Arafat given a hero's welcome in Gaza, all because he said no to Israel's offers of peace."[50]

Yet the explanation of the media's role is not enough to explain the repercussions of Camp David on the cultural elite of the Left and the great reversal that took place. Ehud Barak probably offered Arafat more than any of his predecessors in the Israeli government ever had. The fact that he was ready to accept a retreat from 88% of the occupied territories at the beginning of the talks, and even to split Jerusalem (the Arab part, of course) at the end, promoted the image of a brave leader dedicated to peace, ready to break one of the great taboos of Israeli political culture. Few intellectuals wished to remember that during his short tenure, construction in the colonies grew more than in any prior period. And few wanted to measure the exact size of the territories that he had offered the Palestinians. Was territorial continuity respected? Was the Israeli demand to keep sovereignty over the Esplanade of the Mosques (above the Temple Mount) legitimate enough in light of the real use of the site by believers, given that Jewish tradition has long forbidden access to the site?

Even fewer asked why Israel had the right to further territory beyond the initial 1947 borders, which already gave it control of 77% of the Palestine Mandate. We should also remember that Israeli intellectuals of the greater Left block, in formal opposition to the positions of the various Labor governments and the Israeli public, had long disapproved of the implantation process in the territories. However, when the "final" negotiations with the Palestinians occurred, they showed much more goodwill to Israeli transgression of the 1967 border than to the possibility of Palestinian mobility towards the inside. In other words, keeping large swaths of implantations in the occupied territories was a given, while the return of the Palestinian refugees of 1948 to the State of Israel was unthinkable.

Even if the Israeli denial of the right of return is comprehensible when considering the three and a half million refugees and their descendants—which would de facto abolish the existence of the State of Israel—the lack of understanding and the complete imperviousness to this aspect of the conflict seen in intellectuals who defend peace remain an enigma. Ehud Barak's utter refusal to recognize, even partially, the historical responsibility of Israel in creating the refugee problem and his inflexibility towards the integration of a reasonable number of refugees—which would not pose a threat to the cultural morphology of Israel but symbolize the recognition of wrongs caused—were accepted as obvious and justified by almost all intellectuals on the Left.

The crux of the problem lay in the hypothesis long accepted by this block that final peace could be constructed on the territorial division of the Israeli conquests in 1967. It implied the certainty that Palestinians could be required to forget their past and the drama of 1948 while asking them to accept the memory pragmatically through the daily reminder of the major settlements. Jewish-Israeli intellectual sensibility, anchored in the memory of a "long-term" historical past connected to the "Land of Israel" easily erased the "other's" right to a "short-term" historical memory. For the Left block of intellectuals, the future peace accords would also reflect, in one way or another, the relationships of military power in the field: the strongest should impose and the weakest should accept. The refusal of the Palestinians to accept these conditions took the intellectuals by surprise. The violent uprising in 2000, which gained support from the large protests organized by Israeli Arabs, was a shock and led to decisive changes in the perception of possible resolution to the conflict by Israeli cultural agents.

Nathan Zach, one of the great Hebrew poets, considered to be the epitome of the "man of peace," compared Arafat, in a fit of disdain, to "a grandmother driving a bus without wheels," adding that it was time to remove him. The philosopher Yirmiyahu Yovel joined him by saying that "Arafat apparently has no qualms in sacrificing hundreds of victims for the sake of a propaganda war." Gershon Shaked, one of the leading intellectuals of the peace camp, a literature specialist at the Hebrew University of Jerusalem, thought that the project of partitioning the "Land of Israel" should be maintained but that security considerations should prevail, so that the border should go "a little further east than what is currently being discussed."[51]

Benny Morris went even further. As a researcher who published an important book in the late 1980s on the refugee problem[52] and was a conscientious objector, he reached the conclusion after the Camp David summit that the Palestinians were to blame for whatever happened to them: they were the ones who started the hostilities in every war; they were responsible and therefore had to pay the price. Recognizing that in 1948 a "partial ethnic cleansing" had taken place, Benny Morris considered it retrospectively to be inevitable and justified because it was part of the inherent structure of the creation of the Jewish State. He considered Israel's constant opposition to the return of refugees to be legitimate and even claimed that it would be necessary to conduct a new transfer of the Israeli Arab population since he saw them as a time bomb threatening the security of the country. As for the Palestinians in the occupied territories, he stated: "they should be put away somewhere, like in a cage [...]. There is a wild animal there that must be locked up one way or another."[53]

Statements as crude as those of Benny Morris should not be attributed to all intellectuals on the Left shrouded in deception, but he is an extreme example of a relatively widely-shared state of mind among the Israeli intelligentsia. It was one of the historic moments where the thought of most "major" intellectuals echoed not only the intelligentsia but also the dominant opinions among the masses. This kind of ideological consensus between intellectuals and simple citizens only existed during times of war, at least at the beginning. And there was a war. The Second Intifada, started by Ariel Sharon's visit to the Esplanade of the Mosques in September 2000, began with protests that were forcefully repressed but that quickly turned into an armed struggle culminating in the cruel wave of suicide attacks carried out by Palestinians against Israeli civilians.

The rare intellectuals whose positions were not changed by the crisis of the talks and the outbreak of the new revolt came mainly from what the media labeled the "Post-Zionists." For them, the government of Ehud Barak did not want to understand the profound nature of the conflict and was therefore unable to find a solution. Israel had not entered the negotiations with a spirit of equality between the parties and had not even tried to create the illusion of equality. In the final stage of the negotiations (held in January 2001 in Taba, Sinai), when Barak reached a possible formula for compromise, it was with the knowledge that his government had already run its course. One month later, he handed over the reins to

Ariel Sharon. Israeli society had voted en masse for the "strong man" who could finally put down the Palestinian insurrection.

Yossi Beilin was the only establishment politician to come out of the failed negotiations without suffering too much damage. A man of the Left, a protégé of Shimon Peres since the Oslo Accords, and holder of a doctorate in political science from Tel Aviv University, he was the Minister of Justice in Ehud Barak's government. When the Right returned to power in 2001, and unlike the rest of the political class and in particular intellectuals, he did not give up hope in his Palestinian friends and began a "long march" that ended with the Geneva Accords in 2003 (accords that were concluded between independent political formations, and not between governments).

The intellectual sphere, for the most part, had mixed reactions to the Geneva Accords, which stipulated, for the first time and without ambiguity, that the future borders between Israel and Palestine would be those of 1967, with a possibility of territorial exchange, and that East Jerusalem (the Arab section of the city), with the Esplanade of the Mosques, would be placed under Palestinian sovereignty. Yet while Arafat implicitly approved these texts, Ehud Barak and Shlomo Ben Ami, the former leaders of Israel, refused them completely. The Geneva Accords confirmed that Ehud Barak had not "given everything" to the Palestinians. And they comforted in part the opinion of the groups of marginal intellectuals who had criticized the display of arrogance by the Israeli delegation during the negotiations. Another event would soon shift political lines in the intellectual domain.

In September, one of the main newspapers published a letter signed by twenty-seven combat pilots of the Israeli Air Force as a petition to the public.[54] The petition of protest was invented by French intellectuals at the end of the 19th century to promote their involvement in the public arena. In Israel, it was also often used by people of letters to affirm their collective presence in the agora. In the 1980s, the War in Lebanon elicited the publication of several petitions by reserve soldiers proclaiming their refusal to serve in the occupied territories. However, there had never been a collective refusal by combat pilots, who were considered the elite of the Israeli Army (Tsahal), and in a sense of society as a whole. The pilots, as conscientious objectors, denounced the illegal and amoral character of numerous military operations carried out in the territories and declared that continued occupation would lead to the corruption of Israeli society. Three months later, thirteen elite soldiers from a commando unit reporting directly to military headquarters added their names to the pilots' petition. Their unit was also considered to be one of the Army's most prestigious; Ehud Barak and Benjamin Netanyahu each served in it.

These expressions of disobedience, although they came from a small minority, made waves in the leading sectors of the country. In this militarized society where martial prestige often serves as a springboard for election to the highest political functions, the pilots' actions struck a heavy blow: the arms of the leaders were suddenly being turned against them. The entire political spectrum, from Left to Right, except for a small non-Zionist minority, panicked and immediately branded this act of "high treason." A majority of intellectuals were also shaken and they distanced themselves from this "antipatriotic" and "antidemocratic" act. Some writers, such as Amos Oz and A.B. Yehoshua, declared that only a court of law was able to judge the illegality of an order. Others were afraid to go outside the limits of public legitimacy. Confronting the combat pilots and elite soldiers determined to engage in a public action, which was usually the prerogative of intellectuals, was not an easy role to play. The arguments of the conscientious objectors were primarily based on ethical values and were further emphasized by the fact that some of them paid dearly for their stance: unlike traditional intellectuals, the pilots on active service were dismissed and saw their careers ruined.[55]

Support for the disobedience was at first limited to one major intellectual: Yeshayasu Leibowitz. He was soon followed, with a few reservations, by S. Yizhar, a renowned writer of the 1948 generation, as well as by the writers David Grossman and Sami Michael, poets Nathan Zach and Daliah Rabikovitch, and playwright Yehoshua Sobol.[56] The dam soon burst: dozens of academics crossed the Rubicon to sign a petition in support of the intractable soldiers. The wave made eminent intellectuals on the Zionist Left feel uneasy, and they were slowly swept up by the current, although not without hesitating. The pilots were celebrated but also warned about the implication of their gesture on the future political culture of Israel: what would happen if soldiers influenced by ideology on the Right decided to refuse orders if the terrorists retreated?

It is still too early to analyze all of the reasons that led Ariel Sharon, the major architect of colonization, to decide in 2005 to pull Israeli forces from Gaza and dismantle the settlements that had been built there. How much international pressure was involved? Was the objective of retreat from Gaza to consolidate the settlements in the West Bank and preserve Jerusalem? Dov Weissglass, a close advisor of Sharon, declared that the Geneva Accords had created the climate for this approach and, along with the pilots' letter, contributed to the decision.[57] The Palestinian war of attrition also caused a crack in the vision of a "Greater Israel" and diminished its credibility with a majority of Israelis since fatigue with the prolonged, bloody conflict was felt not only by Palstinians but also in every Israeli home.

An analysis of the statements made by different intellectuals in the context of the retreat from Gaza, however, reveals a key ideological pillar to this new approach, one that gave it a determinant intellectual legitimacy and may have also been its principal motivation. The fear created by the demographic relationship of forces that was behind colonization and its development for almost 40 years gained a larger place in Israeli intellectual discourse. The fear of the cannons and rockets that threatened the existence of Israel in the 1960s and 1970s was replaced by a fear of the fecundity of Palestinian women, which threatened to become a greater threat to the "Jewish State" or more precisely to the "Jewishness" of the State.

The difficulties that Israeli intellectuals on the left first had in supporting the political approach of Ariel Sharon quickly diminished and were often replaced by signs of admiration. The recurring argument in their interviews and articles was that continued occupation could abolish the "Jewish identity" of the State because Israel would be obliged to give the right to vote to Arabs in the territories. To save "Jewish democracy," it became imperative to pull out of "most" of the territories, even without an accord, which is exactly the approach adopted by Ariel Sharon.[58]

It seems possible today to state, albeit with a measure of prudence, that the intellectual debate on the fate of the territory conquered in 1967 is reaching its end. This does not yet mean that the pursuit of the colonial folly, on both political and military levels, is over. The victims, Palestinian in the majority and Israeli, continue to be buried, but in the Israeli cultural sphere only a tiny minority thinks that Israel can maintain direct control over the Palestinian people.

However, the real debate over the meaning of a "Jewish State" or a "State of the Jewish people" and its contradiction with the republican idea of a democracy belonging to all of its citizens has only just begun.[59]

Hath Not a Jew Eyes?

A year before the First Intifada, in 1986, the film *Avanti Popolo* was released by Israeli director Raffi Bukai to great success. The hero, played by Arab-Israeli actor Salim Dau, is an Egyptian soldier abandoned in the Sinai desert during the 1967 War and captured by the Israeli army. As a civilian, the man is an intelligent professional actor and in the key scene of the film, he declaims before the unsophisticated Israelis the famous tirade by Shylock: "Hath not a Jew eyes?" The ignorant Israeli soldiers do not understand and make fun of him.

These soldiers do not appear in Claude Lanzmann's documentary on the Israeli army. They are fictional characters, after all, born of the "fanciful" imagination of a young director educated in Israel and not from real tank officers or heroic and patriotic combat pilots, like in *Tsahal*, the film of a Frenchman of Jewish origin.

It goes without saying that the Israeli director had more success than the Parisian intellectual in his attempt to analyze the normalization made possible by the Zionist revolution of one part of the "descendants of the people of the Book" who, in historic times of trouble, preferred land to words.

But this normalization, or this collective assimilation in modernity, also made it possible for this Israeli filmmaker to film it without illusions.

2

Words That Think Through Us

I therefore claim to show, not how men think in myths, but how myths operate in men's minds without their being aware of the fact.
—Claude Lévi-Strauss, *The Raw and the Cooked*, 1964.

Those who pass among fleeting words, carry your names and be gone.
—Mahmoud Darwish, "Passers between the Passing Words," 1988.

Each person's existence is divided between words and things. Things are always words as well, and words tend to approach things without quite reaching them. When Heidegger wrote that words are thought through people, he forgot to add that intellectuals could sometimes change their meaning in such a way that they become something new. All writing civilizations have given a privileged status to erudite people who could control the neutral zone of the imagination between words and things, or more precisely between written words and the social practices behind their creation. During the major struggles to ensure control over things, intellectuals and people of letters became the main strategists in the art of attributing meaning to the signs and syntax of language, thanks to their mastery of writing.

Their carnal relationship with writing has sometimes led to intellectual conceptions that turn words into a world-creating demiurge. The sages of Talmudic tradition understood that life and death sometimes hung on a word. In the dystopia of his famous novel *1984*, George Orwell showed with deft insight the importance of words in a dark future society and their major role in the advent of totalitarian threats.

In the recent past, trendy American intellectuals decreed that changing words was sufficient to become "politically correct" and that reality would also change as a result. These new norms of language inherited a normative and moral function to maintain order and to stigmatize deviants. As a general rule, the most significant linguistic evolution was confined to universities and the circles of the cultural elite, according to an intellectual approach that contributed to masking traditional class differences and comfortable discriminatory cultural practices applied without hesitation in the real world. Changing words took the place of a more complex project in many cases: changing the order of things—a project that failed many times over the course of the 20th century.

Words do not walk alone: they are always hand in hand with the evasive, adult hand of things. It would be naïve to think that forming and creating new words and their existence in linguistic culture only have a negligible influence on how the consciousness of social groups is formed. If ways of thinking condition the choice of words, these words also condition ways of thinking in return and create new frameworks for perceiving reality. In fact, words are not born within us but we are born into words. The formulas of language shape our thoughts from birth.

Words do not create social relationships of force, even though there are no relationships of force without the appropriate expressions. While social relationships have often served in history as an arena for political combats with decisive influence in determining relationships of power and dependence, words have always served as weapons or armor in these campaigns. The intellectual elite, with logistical support from the political elite, has always excelled in mobilizing words and language, even if, in one way or another, the political elite has always known how to impose its will during the decisive moments of a battle.[1]

In the case of the Zionist revolution, words were the cornerstone for building the new Jewish nation: the conquest of land to turn it into a national good found solid support in the elaboration and diffusion of a rich and varied linguistic culture. Many of the first immigrants already knew some Hebrew before coming to Palestine; however, most of the immigrants from Europe who came later were obliged to emigrate from one language to another. The Hebrew language itself grew richer and changed over time. New words were invented and added, while others were labeled "archaic" and were neglected and abandoned. An entire category of words with strong ideological and political meanings was fixed and preserved with help from intellectuals, the guards at the gates of the language. All those who hesitated in using these words were labeled the sworn enemies of national resurrection.

Linguistic Mythologies

The Zionist movement told the story of its colonization by means of a systematic rewriting of the names of places, people and fundamental universal concepts. "Soft" words were translated into powerful linguistic mythologies. The particular attention that the intellectual and political elite paid to the centrality of language in building the national consciousness was not specific to Zionism; similar phenomena took place in other national cultures.[2] Zionism's specificity lies in its combination of a national movement and colonization. The relationship between the intellectual avant-garde and immigrant populations was different than those observed between the elite and the masses in most other national cultures of the 19th and 20th centuries. This relationship also led to the production of a fascinating, but problematic political language. The formation of the Jewish national consciousness was not only anchored in the imagination of a past punctuated by new words but also in a national present that relied on the massive production of specific signifiers, mainly in connection with the slow process of acquiring territorial space.

Analyzing the "politically correct" in the Zionist language developed by several generations of Hebrew, then Israeli intellectuals raises a number of questions: Is it possible to use Modern Hebrew, with its basic concepts, to write a history of Zionism that is not by necessity a Zionist historiography? Will literature, poetry and journalistic essays always be caught in the very specific conceptual mechanisms created in the context of mobilization that began with the building of the national culture? Is the vocabulary of Modern Hebrew necessarily subject to the internal codes of the ideological semantic planning that created it and will the language always be its prisoner?

These questions should not suggest that it is possible to give definitive answers. Hebrew will continue to develop and evolve according to the ideological processes that will decide the character of its future culture and it is difficult to say what direction they will take. At this stage, however, it is possible to engage in a critical analysis of the political recruitment of "innocent" words. It would be futile to think that a greater awareness of their ideological weight would mean escaping their influence completely. Nonetheless, a heightened awareness could contribute to words being a little less thought through people and to people thinking a little more through words.

To illustrate the ways ideology interferes with words, which only appear to respond to a pure informative logic, I will use a Hebrew sentence that has many variants in the history books used in Israeli public schools as well as in university research, canonical novels and news articles: *Haim Nahman Bialik natach ett ha-Galut ve-Ala le-Eretz Israel chanim meatot lifnay Praot tarpat*. The English translation is as follows: "Haim Nahman Bialik left Exile and rose to the Land of Israel a few years before the pogroms of the year 5689."

This typical sentence gives biographical information about the renowned Hebrew poet and also information on his destination. Every famous Israeli intellectual—historian, journalist or writer—who has imagined or written about the common past expresses him- or herself using the same or similar words, and constantly produces words in this style without thinking about them.

I will start with a deconstruction of the sentence to propose an alternative utterance that may draw out a new reflexive relationship between the reader and the collective memory that contains the components of his or her identity. Writing that aspires to use the mechanisms of more universal concepts is one of the preconditions for the development of a more open and peaceful climate in Israel, as well as for theoretical reflection that transcends conjectural theoretical debate. In the end, intellectuals are not supposed to be directly involved in politics—it is better to leave it to the politicians. But they must remember that, despite the historical erosion of their status and prestige, they retain, given their ethical responsibility, a privileged place with surplus value in the production of the fundamental symbols with which a culture is made and developed. We can only agree with Amos Oz, who in his attempt to define one of the roles of the intellectual, wrote:

> And because writers are, or at least should be, specialists in nuances—their role requires them to show discernment [...]. We invent, deform, exaggerate, twist things inside out and upside down. But as soon as we formulate things in words—our words become witnesses. This is our responsibility in terms of nuances and discernment.

Ha-Galut: "Exile"

The *Galut* or *Gola* (exile)[3] left by Bialik is a term used by Zionist language and clearly inspired by religious vocabulary. "Exile" was one of the key elements in the self-determination of Jewish identity and marked its limits. A detailed analysis of the concept's various significations in different Jewish traditions is beyond the scope of this discussion.[4] I will simply note that the traditional religious meaning of the term "exile" went far beyond the immediate definition generally attributed to it: being forced to stay outside one's country of origin. The temporal dimension in the concept of "exile" according to Mosaic Law is completely different than the contingence implied in the secular concept of exile. Moreover, the term was used as one of the expressions of Jewish identity as opposed to the Christian state of grace granted to the world by Jesus' arrival among humankind. Jewish religiousness in its various forms saw "exile" as the expression of divine judgment causing people a metaphysical, purifying suffering that would end with Redemption.

It is one of the reasons, but not the only one, that Jewish people throughout history have not left their place of origin, have not renounced their local culture, have not abandoned the graves of their ancestors and have not tried to leave, of their own accord, for Zion. Even during the Caliphate, when Babylon and Jerusalem were under a unified temporal power, the many Jews in Babylon did not attempt to end their "forced exile" and preferred immigrating to Baghdad. The Jews cast out of Spain settled in the cities of "exile" in the Mediterranean basin, and only a few pushed all the way to the Holy City, which at first glance did not seem to be in "exile." (Was it always this way? Jewish people have always lived in the Holy Land, in other words, not in "exile," yet they adopted almost the same mode of existence as the "exiled"!) Despite their prayers, which were a constant expression of their attachment to the Holy Land, Jews did not emigrate to Jerusalem (except for a few isolated mystics and exalted messianic movements); at most, they would go on a pilgrimage or be buried there.

Taking into consideration the specific characteristics of Judaism as compared to the other monotheistic religions, and despite the special place occupied by Jerusalem, there is a somewhat uncomfortable but not completely inaccurate comparison to be made in the fact that Muslims have not emigrated to Mecca and Christians have never expressed the idea of moving to Rome. A faith's holy land has always been a religious and messianic pole of attraction but has never been a national homeland to which the faithful had to "return." This has not prevented the priests and believers of each of these religions from trying to exercise control over their holy sites.

The new national intellectual minority, which adopted religious semantics and put them at the heart of the nationalized holy language, knew the stakes involved and zealously pursued this approach. The instrumentalization of traditional religious vocabulary did not mean that intellectuals did not believe in the phraseology they created: the founders of a new myth often become its first adepts. Zionist intellectuals made "exile" a fundamental mental category with two objectives: 1) to serve as a conceptual foundation for a secular entity that would define Jewish communities as a people and as a nation since the destruction of the First Temple; 2) to prevent planning a collective future in the territorial space where the Jews of the Yiddish people continued to live.

It must be noted, however, that this secular and radical intellectual minority went against all contemporary currents of thought and political movements, which did not see themselves as living in "exile." Most intellectuals of Jewish origin, having contributed alternative ideologies to the declining religious orthodoxy, generally refused to secularize religious categories. As for the European intellectuals who had taken their distances from the Jewish religion, and in some cases completely abandoned it (such as Enlightenment thinkers and, later, liberals, anarchists, social democrats, communists, members of the Bund and other autonomists), they all expressed important critiques of different aspects of Jewish life but never saw life in European countries as a form of "exile." From their perspective, in general, their country of origin all too often rejected them and made their integration difficult; but they were also supposed to get used to the idea of a Jewish presence that would evolve and end up being integrated in a more enlightened world.

We can also note that the majority of the Jewish masses (and not just the intellectual elite) that began their great push to the West for economic reasons of persecution did not see themselves as "exiles" either. Their constant efforts to integrate into their new societies did not coincide with the secular and alienating perception of "exile." "Exile," therefore, in its modern, non-religious definition, was not a "Jewish" concept at all but an almost uniquely Zionist one.

The first Zionist intellectuals put the concept of "exile" at the heart of their ideological program and started the political rallying cry to end it. The agents of Zionist, then Israeli culture have repeated it for almost a century. While it has lost some of its original power of attraction, we cannot say that it has been removed from the dominant Hebrew lexicon. The most eminent Israeli sociologists, historians and philosophers still use the term "exile" as if it defined an existing historical reality and as if its end were a definitive conclusion to a prior period of national history.

Even if it is easy to understand that a movement with the goal of encouraging its members to abandon a place of danger in order to gather in an independent territory (and its appreciation of history was later revealed to be justified) needed a myth to mobilize them; even if it is delusional to dismiss the idea that this term provided mental support for many immigrants in helping them overcome the painful process of leaving their culture of origin; even if it is legitimate to think that any attempt to get around the concept would block access to several aspects of the spiritual world of Zionist intellectuals; even when we admit the validity of all of these arguments, there would still be the difficulty of understanding how this linguistic myth, in its modern definition, is used in all of the research and literary texts in Hebrew that deal with the history of the Jewish people through time.

Examples abound in hundreds of books of research: when the prominent historian Shmuel Almog of the Hebrew University of Jerusalem writes with perfect scientific seriousness about "the movements that defended Jewish autonomy in exile in different ways,"[5] he integrates the autonomists into a discursive structure conditioned by a Zionist view of history and distances Israeli readers from an understanding of the context in which this autonomism developed. If the Bundists, for example, had thought that the Jews living in the Russian Empire were in "exile," they would have become Zionists, and Almog would not have had to treat it as an independent political movement.

The common use of the term "exile" represents not only an anachronistic discursive practice, it is also an obstacle to understanding the conditions of existence of the Yiddish people in Eastern Europe or the ways in which other Jewish communities perpetuated themselves. It also undermines any serious attempt to decode the processes of secularization, modernization and politicization as well as to analyze the social relationships experienced by Jewish people in different cultures and societies. The most harmful aspect is the "scientific" use of the term "exile" in a chain of remodeled concepts that perpetuates and reproduces the vision of the Jews as an "ethnicity" with immutable biological traits, uprooted from their country of origin in Antiquity and condemned to wander in suffering and abandon, ever erring like the Flying Dutchman in the hostility of the seas.

It is disturbing to contemplate the extent to which some of the fundamental characteristics of modern anti-Semitism have rubbed off on the definition given by the "authorized" intellectuals of Jewish historical thought and the Zionist national idea. It is just as worrisome to note how these values are perpetuated in Israeli culture. The new "ethno-biological" anti-Semites who appeared in the second half of the 19th century as distinct from the traditional anti-Jewish Christians began to see themselves as the direct descendants of Aryans or Indo-Europeans that came from northern India to the European continent. We can imagine that if the adepts of this idea saw themselves as a persecuted cultural minority in Europe, they would have also developed a propensity for the feeling of modern "exile" and perhaps even nostalgia for their original "Indian homeland."

At a certain point in history, too many European intellectuals who claimed to represent a majority united by a common ethnic origin that was the first to arrive in Europe. To consolidate and solidify their new, still unstable national identities, they attributed to others the status of uninvited "ethnicities" on a continent that was at the time one of the richest zones of development in the world. Evolutionist scientists also contributed to the formation of this successful ideological perversion, which created the conditions of a new "exile" for all of these "others," of different cultural and religious traditions.

The Jewish concept of "exile," inspired by the religious tradition as we have seen, also underwent a radical change with the developments in the new sciences and their "influence" on the cultural environment. The old tribal myth of the "seed of Abraham," vestiges of which were preserved in Jewish religious rituals, became a "Jewish scientific truth." From there, the concept of "exile" began to introduce the idea that Jews of the modern era were the direct biological descendants of the "Children of Israel." These Semites uprooted from their ancestral lands spread throughout the world at a surprising rate (especially with the fall of the Roman Empire). Since the "Children of Israel" in Antiquity represented not only a religious community but also a people with a common origin, the followers of Judaism who survived over the next eighteen centuries began to be considered by racist anti-Semites, and also by intellectuals of Jewish origin, as a group from a "race" that was foreign to the Aryan peoples. The invention of the two thousand year-old "Jewish people" had begun.

Moses Hess, one of the most incisive and fascinating intellectuals of the 19th century, served as the first impetus in the secular transmission between linguistic, then racist Indo-European expansion and the development of a concept that gave Jews the status of an exiled foreign "ethnicity" in Europe. In 1862, he wrote in his captivating essay *Rome and Jerusalem*: "Jewish noses cannot be reformed, and the black, wavy hair of the Jews will not change through conversion into blond, nor can its curves be straightened out by constant combing. The Jewish race is one of the primary races of mankind that has retained its integrity, in spite of the continual change of its climatic environment, and the Jewish type has conserved its purity through the centuries."[6]

It is not by chance that *Rome and Jerusalem* is considered to be one of the first works in the birth and elaboration of Jewish national thought. In this book by the man who may have been the first Zionist thinker, the concept of "son of Israel" stopped applying to communities of believers whose common points had always been reduced to religious cultural norms and began to designate an "ethno-biological nation," an atemporal entity which had preserved itself through history by the miracle of "election." "Exile" in the secular sense is a painful and unbearable situation fundamentally represented by the image of forced separation from a natural environment and forced presence in a place of alienation. The same image was used again eighty-five years after the publication of Moses Hess' book in the Declaration of the Establishment of the

State of Israel: "After being forcibly exiled from their land, the people kept faith with it throughout their Dispersion...."

This mythological representation of a martyred people intended to close the parenthesis of the "Dispersion" that had occurred two thousand years before. The way in which the boundaries of the identity of the "people" were defined in the eyes of the national project's secular leaders is no secret: all voluntary integration was eliminated from the definition of the collective identity, and national leaders finally settled on the principle of religious exclusivity, according to which only people of a Jewish mother or who had converted according to ancestral tradition belonged to the "Jewish nation."

However, the Zionist cultural elite had long stopped seeing Judaism as a religion full of vigor and complexity that would grow, convert individuals and entire kingdoms with ease, produce a diversity of cultures and gather human groups of different origins together in the belief in a single God. This historical Judaism, which in its decline had left the Yiddish people behind in Eastern Europe, contributed to the birth and the identity of the new Israeli nation despite the orthodoxy of its source. Yet the intellectuals who pioneered the nation saw it as a single, ahistorical essentialism that endured because of the "ethnic" stock common to all of the faithful and not because of its religious dimension. As the history of Jewish communities was not able to prove the existence of secular cultural practices and norms shared by all (language, clothing, music, food...), national thinkers were forced to rely on a biological essence.[7]

The lack of a common popular culture among all descendants of the Jews throughout the world led Zionist intellectuals to pay more attention and show more sensitivity to the ancient ethnic "origin" than to the forms of revelation of the "Jewish essence" even in "exile." This preconceived notion was held by all those who rejected "exile," from Vladimir (Ze'ev) Jabotinsky, the leader of the Right, to Ber Borochov, the father of Zionist Marxism. Jabotinsky did not hesitate to state that "by eliminating all of the successive strata accumulated from historical conditions, climate, natural environment and the influence of foreign peoples, the nation will be reduced, in the end, to its radical element."[8] Borochov, on the other hand, displayed great disdain for the philosophers of race, but because his rejection of "exile" was no less vehement, he let himself be convinced—an archetype of the leftist Zionist—that the racial composition of the indigenous populations of Palestine was closer to the Jewish people than to any other: "It would seem that the racial difference between a Jew in exile and Palestinian farmers is no greater than the one that distinguishes Ashkenazy and Sephardim Jews."[9]

We could cite other leading thinkers of Zionism, from Max Nordau, the brilliant essayist who wrote of the "ties of blood existing between the members of the Israelite family," to Arthur Ruppin, the pacifist intellectual who organized colonization in the Palestinian Mandate, who thought that "the racial configuration of the majority of Jews [who survived] resembles their ancestors in the ancient land of Israel."[10] However, these nationalist intellectuals and their terminology deserve some indulgence: even if many of them had an essentialist conception of Jewishness, harking back to a single biological-territorial origin, preserving the "purity of the race" for most was never part of their program (the Jewish religion, despite the ancient ethno-tribal myth of a common founding father that it carries with it, did not allow this type of approach). We must also remember that until the Second World War, use of the word "race" was widespread and popular in many intellectual circles. Zionists were part of a larger family of thought that comprised the classic racist Right, free-market thinkers and even socialists.

After the Second World War, the more elusive and vague term "ethnicity" slowly began to replace "race" because it was much more neutral and "easier" to use in "scientific" intellectual discourse about the origins of human groups. Israeli universities pursue research from time to time to attempt to discover the Jewish gene that is common to the descendants of communities from the Ukraine, Morocco and Yemen. But DNA has remained a scientific tool that has yet to cooperate with the imperatives of Jewish ethnic thought.

The Jewish ethnic essentialism that was so important to Zionist intellectuals and without which, they thought, their territorial claims on the "land of Israel" would lack legitimacy, was insufficient from the start. The "negation of *Galut* [exile]" in Zionist language not only means the total removal of non-national Jewish existence from "exile" but also the negation of the "exile mentality" from which Jewish essence suffered. This intention also reflected the way in which many Zionist intellectuals integrated the parameters of the new ethnic anti-Semitism. "Exile" (*Galut*) and the "exile mentality" (*Galutiut*) have always had a pejorative sense and these terms designate the Jewish people stripped of sovereignty. Obviously, the Zionist border patrol was obliged to detect and confiscate this incriminating baggage when crossing the frontiers of national rebirth. The dishonorable Jewish essence was part of the culture and the mentality of the Yiddish people that Zionism was supposed to liberate, at the cost of erasing its real identity. Since visual imagination is often more blunt and transparent than conceptual imagination, we only have to look at the posters for Hebrew films from the 1930s and 40s to see how Zionist culture pictured the ideal "non-exiled" man and woman (Moses Hess would surely object to the straight hair and "Aryan" noses).

One could have expected that the use of the word "exile" would have disappeared from the latest generation of the Israeli intelligentsia, which started to question the lack of sensibility and understanding of the "non Jewish other" and the national-militarist heroism that was considered necessary for Israeli society in its beginnings. This expectation is heightened by the renewed presence of intellectuals of Jewish origin in American culture who are reactivating expressions of cultural specificity that are supposed to be disappearing and also by the weight of pro-Israeli figures in Western politics who make no secret of their Jewishness. These elements could have, in one way or another, made Israeli intellectuals more reticent towards the univocal negation of "exile." Restoring vigor to "exiled" existence is now fashionable and is not harmful as long as the use of the expression continues to enhance the prestige of Israeli Jews and confirms their centrality to Jewish culture outside Israel.

Let there be no mistake: the negative and purifying power of the word continues to create new meanings and be adopted by school book writers or journalists who are out of touch with prevailing sentiment. Take, for example, the programmatic article by Assa Kasher, philosophy professor at Tel-Aviv University and universally recognized as a prominent Israeli intellectual. At the turn of the century in 2000, he was asked to describe the Zionist ideal at the end of the second millennium:

It is very difficult to move beyond the exile of the Jewish people, even in Israel. But, despite everything, it is still possible to move forward, to reach the top of the mountain. In this context, Zionism in the year 2000 means greater personal restraint in our daily lives, for example while driving.[11]

I am not sure whether this "exile mentality" that causes so many Jews to die in car accidents should make us laugh or cry. It goes to show how intellectual history—to borrow the words of another "Jew-in-exile" named Marx—repeats itself, first as tragedy and then as farce.

Coming back to Bialik, we should remember that the "national poet" himself did not rush to leave behind his sad and alienating "exile" in Ukraine, his distant country of birth, or the "exile mentality" at the heart of his work. It took Soviet dictatorship eliminating all possibility of independent literary creation in Hebrew to force him to leave the land of his "exiled" childhood and youth for Berlin. Sadly, this city, in 1921, was not destined to become a center of Hebrew literature. Three years later, he decided to join the "Fourth Ascent."

Ha'Aliyah: The "Ascent"

Use of the Hebrew word *Aliyah* (ascent) to refer to "emigration" to the country containing the point of lowest elevation in the continental world reveals that one who uses the term holds the traditional belief that sanctifies this land or the specific national myth that gives precedence to the place where the myth becomes reality. Substituting national *Aliyah* for the religious *Aliyah la-regel* (pilgrimage) gave the painful act of being uprooted from "exile" a new radical value. "Exile" was obviously seen as an inferior place, and this representation continued in the "politically correct" Zionist language still in use today. A Jew "ascends" to the "Land of Israel" when he or she immigrates and "descends" from it when he or she leaves.

In fact, a Jew never *immigrates* to Israel. Only foreign workers, non Jews, who decide not to return to their country of origin, become clandestine immigrants (their children born in Israel who live there for years can never become Israeli citizens and are also defined as illegal immigrants). Those who are identified as Jews, on the other hand, according to scientific works of history and sociology, fictional novels, poems and songs, data from the Ministry of the Interior and daily language are the only ones who can "ascend" to Israel, the place from which they "descended" only two thousand years ago.

Until now, Israeli intellectuals have felt at ease using Zionist terminology: in foreign publications of texts edited in parallel in the vernacular language, the words *Aliyah* and *Olim* ("those who ascend")—in a convention applied to other words, as we will see later—are translated by "immigration" and "immigrants." Thus historians, geographers, sociologists and writers preserve the "norms of international semantics" without tainting the Hebrew language with non-Zionist terminology. It is also amusing to watch how young Israeli intellectuals considering criticism of Zionism bend to the will of its linguistic hegemony without measuring the reality-shaping power that these terms carry in the national consciousness. This consciousness is ready to weather serious ethical critiques or face uncomfortable factual data rather than revolutionize the entire conceptual structure of the language, which could create independent networks of thought or new types of identities.

In the confusion of the 1990s, and in the new, less welcoming environment for Zionist thought, some Zionist historians and sociologists began to sense the insufficiently "scientific" character of the use of such visibly ideological terms. It led to the very careful appearance of hesitant excuses with the goal, despite all evidence, of preserving the heart of the theoretical structure that proved to be so effective in building the nation. A few examples of this new approach follow.

Yaacov Shavit, one of the most eminent historians of Tel-Aviv University, found it appropriate to state in one of his methodological essays:

> A concept can also sometimes distort facts, although not necessarily. The description of the arrival of the Jews in Israel using the term *Aliyah* instead of immigration, for example, should not prevent a historian from analyzing *Aliyah* as a phenomenon of "immigration."[12]

This proposition might be acceptable if it were not a case of an "obsolete" semantic use of a word with an original meaning that has completely lost and forgotten its mythological influence. Words sometimes change their meaning and lose their former meanings. But Yaacov Shavit is not a secret non-Zionist historian who believes in the advent of a post-Zionist era where Zionist words have completely lost their inspirational power.

This experienced scholar knows full well that he lives in a world of semantic politics where *Aliyah*, despite the anti-ideological skepticism introduced in the 1990s, is still considered to be a positive, valued historical action (even when it refers to non-ideological immigration from Eastern Europe). It is totally legitimate that Yaacov Shavit, as a citizen, chooses to defend this political position, but as a historian he cannot deny that the mythical aspect of this term is still "hot" and lively, and still participates in diverse strata of Israeli political culture. Its use in historical and sociological research there-fore represents a deliberate act to conserve the values it represents, which still have the power to direct the modes of perception of its referent in contemporary historical reality.

Here is another example of an attempt to preserve Zionist seman-tics at all cost: when Aviva Halamish, another historian of Zionism, decided to examine the different perceptions of Jewish immigration methods into the Palestinian Mandate in the 1930s, her abstract explained how the term *Aliyah* carried heavy meaning and values that were connected to pre-Zionist religious sources.[13] Aviva Halamish chose to follow a mode of conduct consisting of "using the most com-mon terms in the society that the research examines and in the language of the article." This rule allowed her to assure her readers that in presenting the position of the Arabs or the British on the issue, she would have used the universal term "immigration."

Readers with a critical mind would have some difficulty under-standing why the historian was supposed to use the term *Aliyah*, with its highly-charged value, when discussing Zionist discourse and use the more neutral "immigration" when referring to Arab dis-course. Following the same principle, it would have been just as justified to use "the common term in the society that the research examines" in the case of the Arab population. She should have added, without quotation marks, the expressions "Zionist invasion," "invasion," "occupation," or "Jewish takeover" to convince the reader of the scientific symmetry and impartiality of her method.

Aviva Halamish is not a post-Zionist historian in the full sense of the word. She does not believe in balanced and equal historical narratives in the face of the truth: like many other Israeli historians that preceded her or will follow her, she believes in *her* truth made up of its own Hebrew words, and not words that are a little more "universal" that aspire to a truth that is independent of national discourse—a truth that may remain unreachable as a whole but one that cannot abandon the universal principle inherent in its definition.

Eretz Israel: The "Land of Israel"

At the beginning of his exciting research into *The Emergence of the Palestinian-Arab National Movement*, Yehoshua Porath, a leading Orientalist from the Hebrew University of Jerusalem, encountered the same semantic problem and decided to adopt a similar approach:

> I have used the term "Land of Israel" to designate the territory studied in this research even though it carries a negative ideological connotation for Arabs in the country. It is the Hebrew name of the country and the language of the predominant narrative. However, I have avoided using this term when transcribing the words of Arabs and, *a fortiori*, when direct quotations are given.[14]

This apparently measured and serious approach is a step forward in the long march towards the secularization of the Hebrew language. Ya'acov Barnai, another important historian, expressed himself in similar terms in his work *Historiography and Nationalism*:

> Another question concerns the name of the territory. We know that the Jewish name is the "Land of Israel" and this name has been used in Jewish historiography and various Jewish publications. But the community of nations and believers in other religions call it "Palestine" from the name "Plesheth," while

Arab-Muslims, with the rise of Palestinian-Arab nationalism in the early 20th century call it "Falastin."[15]

In Hebrew, the "Jewish name" of the territory in question is the "Land of Israel"; and all culture producers, almost without exception, use this term. This common practice, used even by critical Israeli intellectuals, has its justification in the fact that the expression indicates a geographical location that does not necessarily indicate claims or rights of a political nature. It is a strange argument, just as strange as the consensus surrounding it in Israeli culture and intellectual circles.

Naming countries by the name of the peoples who live there or naming peoples by the name of the land they inhabit is common. It is less common to name countries with the name of peoples who no longer inhabit them but who "sojourned" in them two thousand years earlier. No one would call France the "Land of the Celts" or Great Britain the "Land of the Normans." The Danzig region is not called "Land of the Germans" even though Germans have lived there for many years.

The present case is not a translation problem alone, as many Israeli intellectuals would have us and themselves believe. In Hebrew, Spain is called *Sfarad* and its inhabitants are called *Sfaradim*. Israelis call Egypt *Mizraim*, and Egyptians *Mizrim*. The diversity and variety of translations do not carry a subjective ideological charge comparable to the use of the expression "Land of Israel."

Place names have changed throughout history and we can only suppose that they will continue to change in the future. The land of "Canaan" or of "Amor" became the land of "Judea," just as the western part of the greater "Land of Israel" became "Palaestina" and then "Falastin." Although the Arab world has difficulty admitting it, in 1948 the Western part of the Palestinian Mandate became "Israel." From a political point of view, I have the hope that one day, even though it may not be soon, Palestinians will accept the painful fact that Tel Aviv is in Israel and Israelis will recognize that Al-Quds (Jerusalem) is in Palestine. No superior or metaphysical force gave names to the planet's places and lands for all eternity; semantic practices are not a natural phenomenon.

The new Zionist language decided at a certain point that the land stretching from the sea to the desert, from Sinai to Lebanon, would be the land of the Jews and no one else, because they had occupied it two thousand years ago. Because of this, every Hebrew writer was obliged to follow this pseudo-geographical convention. However, calling the Palestinian Mandate of the 1920s "Land of Israel" for this same reason or because British colonialism, in one of its periods of support of Zionism, accepted to add the initials "E'I" (for *Eretz Israel*) to the common name "Palestine" represents a less than neutral essentialism.

We should recognize that the expression "Land of Israel" comes with significant geographical flexibility, just as it did during the writing of the different sections of the Bible. Contrary to what Israeli intellectuals insist, it does not represent the "Hebrew name of the place" because the land surrounding Jerusalem varied in size and had various names in the Bible, the name "Land of Israel" being one of the least common, all things considered. It is logical that the "Hebrew name of the country" does not appear at all in the five books of the Pentateuch, because the "Land of Israel" did not exist yet. The flexible and non-codified Hebrew of the Bible calls it "Canaan" or the "Land of Amor."

We should note that unlike contemporary intellectuals, the erudite sages who compiled the Bible, although their country had been promised to them by God, knew that until the Israelites had settled on the land it could not be called the "Land of Israel," and that it had to carry the name of the people who inhabited it. (Because they had no archaeologists, they did not yet know that the Canaanites, and in fact their fathers, had become faithful servants of Yahweh.) The first mention of the expression Eretz Israel comes in the first Book of Samuel (13:19) and later occurrences are limited—it only appears a dozen times in the entire Bible. "Zion," "Holy Land," "Land of God" or Jerusalem are more commonly used.

The ancestral Jewish use of the expression "Holy Land" entered the new national Hebrew vocabulary which was still written in foreign languages at the beginning. When Leon Pinsker, one of the first intellectuals of Zionism, wrote Auto-Emancipation in 1883, he did not yet know that the "Holy Land" would soon only be called the "Land of Israel." "The goal of our present endeavors must be not the 'Holy Land,' but a land of our own," he declared in his famous essay and "perhaps the Holy Land will again become ours. If so, all the better."[16] The feeling of ownership was not clearly stated yet, and the name was not yet decided. Even the stanzas of *Hatikva* (The Hope), the moving song written by Naftali Herz Imber that became the national anthem of Israel, uses the names "Zion" and "Jerusalem" while the expression "Land of Israel"—the "Jewish" or "Hebrew name" of the place according to Porath, Barnai and hundreds of other producers of referents—does not appear as an object of nostalgic aspiration.

Most of the first intellectuals who followed the Jewish national dream did not write in Hebrew. From Theodore Herzl to Nahman Sirkin, most works named the coveted land "Palaestina." Today, readers of their works in Hebrew will systematically find the expression "Land of Israel." In 1903, during the great debate over the possibility of a Jewish state in Uganda,[17] those who opposed this option were not called "adepts of the Land of Israel" but "Zionists of Zion," "Palestinocentrists," and even "Palestinians." The expression "Land of Israel" that can be found in all of the texts concerning the debates translated into Hebrew profoundly alters the understanding of modern modes of reference to the "land of deliverance" or the "Promised Land." While Israeli erudites call the place "Palestine" in their publications in foreign languages, national logic and the "comfort" of their Hebrew readers leads them to change "Palaestina," the term used by the first Zionists, into "Land of Israel."

The expression "Land of Israel," preferred over all other names, has not always been a banal and anodyne translation. It is the product of a textual codification that is aware of the mobilizing myth and a constant reaffirmation of the "rights of historical ownership of a people without a land over a land without people." When publishing their epochal *Eretz Israel in the Past and the Present* in 1918, David Ben-Gurion and Yitzhak Ben Zvi, despite writing the book in Yiddish, deliberately chose the Hebrew that was best suited to their idea of national ownership. They explain their choice clearly in the conclusion. They had another reason for using a Hebrew expression that was not commonly used at the time, especially by Yiddish readers. These two young, fervent intellectuals who later became major figures in the Zionist project declared in exaltation:

> The Land of Israel must also include El-Arish, although from a political perspective this region is situated outside Turkish Palestine and now belongs to the Egyptians (or more precisely, England). Yet the El-Arish region is fully part of the Land of Israel from a historical and geophysical point of view, and the division between Turkish Palestine and El-Arish is the product

of an artificial border imposed by the Anglo-Egyptian government between Rafah and Aqaba.[18]

Under Ottoman rule, this region (that the "authorized" scholars of
the Hebrew language now call "geographically" the Land of Israel)
did not represent a single administrative entity. Ben-Gurion and Ben
Zvi had elsewhere called it "Turkish Palestine." But in 1917, as
opposed to what happened in the following years, the territorial lim-
itation was considered to be artificial because, "geographically"
speaking, it was too small in the eyes of the two ambitious writers.

In fact, the only entity that was not artificial but "natural-
physical" and therefore corresponded to the historical land registry,
was "Greater Israel," which reached from the Litani River (in
Lebanon) to El-Arish in the South, and from the Mediterranean Sea
to the desert located to the east of Baschan, Golan, Guilad, Amon
and Moab—in other words, the borders of the Promised Land.
When *Eretz Israel* was published, the "Turkish Palestine" referred to
in the book had already been conquered and replaced by the "Palestinian Mandate," which in turn would quickly be considered
artificial because it did not correspond to the "Land of Israel." In the
sophisticated battle of names, however, a first battle had been won:
with the assent of British colonial rule, the initials E'I were added to
the official name of "Palestine" (for "Palestine/Eretz Israel").

> Every indigenous people will resist alien settlers as long as they
> see any hope of ridding themselves of the danger of foreign
> settlement. That is what the Arabs in Palestine are doing, and
> what they will persist in doing as long as there remains a soli-
> tary spark of hope that they will be able to prevent the
> transformation of "Palestine" into the "Land of Israel."[19]

These perceptive sentences from a 1933 essay by Vladimir Jabotinsky entitled "The Iron Wall" expressed his determined position on the problem. Like Ben-Gurion and Ben Zvi, the leader of the Right was also an authentic intellectual with an acute sensitivity for words, especially motivational words. He knew that to control a land you also had to control the words that defined its perimeters.

Fifteen years later, the Declaration of the Establishment of the State of Israel was published, opening with the words of the famous myth: "Eretz Israel was the birthplace of the Jewish people. [...] Impelled by this historic and traditional attachment, Jews strove in every successive generation to re-establish themselves in their ancient homeland." This fundamental semantic structure penetrated the Israeli national consciousness to the point of becoming the only recognized name in the vernacular for this piece of land. But what is this land for which the cultural elite produced these "authorized" words? As we know, the Declaration does not indicate the precise borders of the State of Israel. This omission did not happen by chance. Even if many were ready to accept what they had acquired, a majority clearly felt that the lines of the 1949 ceasefire did not match the frontiers of their "ancient homeland."

One issue remains: anyone who is familiar with the ways in which national identities are formed in the modern era knows that the collective consciousness, in parallel with the definition of the limits of those who participate in it, must also define the territorial borders of its sovereignty. National identity has always included the territorial area that its affiliated members occupy and control in its self-definitions. The land is the exclusive property of the collective national entity, and in the modern national imagina-tion, the power in the feeling of ownership of a particular concrete territory is similar to property rights for private goods, the cornerstone of capitalist civilization. National-territorial thinking began to develop in parallel with the legal consolidation of the modern bourgeois code on private property. And the rise of modern democracy influenced the concept of control of the national territory. When a people realizes that it has sovereignty in its State, State ownership of the national land is seen by citizens as an expression of their direct control.

However, as Benedict Anderson showed in *Imagined Communities*, the borders of pre-modern kingdoms and dynasties and their sovereignty over the territories under their control were generally vague and diluted.[20] Napoleon could sell Louisiana in the early 19th century and the Tsar of Russia could sell Alaska in the middle of the same century, but this type of transaction became unthinkable in the national imagination of the 20th century. Because of the awareness of this inalienable right, since the 1950s it has been possible to dismantle multinational States but practically impossible to move national borders, even by a kilometer.

We can only fully understand the reaction of the most eminent Israeli intellectuals to the conquest of the West Bank in 1967 by understanding this feeling of ownership of the national territory, or the way in which the "Land of Israel" is present in the categories of the national language. It is not surprising, in this light, that political poets like Uri Zvi Grinberg and Nathan Alterman quickly joined the "Greater Israel" movement and their manifestos implored future governments never to abandon even an acre of the land. It is more surprising, however, that moderate writers such as Shai Agnon, Haim Hazaz and many others also joined in the emotions and enthusiasm of the call by intellectuals to annex all of the occupied territories immediately.

The feeling of ownership over the "ancient homeland" brought together various circles of the Israeli intelligentsia because in every form of national modernity, the homeland is one and indivisible. Anyone who would call the whole into question strikes at the national community that lives there. Modern nationalism and not traditional religion, as it may appear, is responsible for the long process of giving Hebrew names to places, cities, territories and for erasing the Green Line that marked the "temporary" borders of the State of Israel until 1967. The deep-set aspiration to have political borders match the borders of national-territorial ownership that is inherent in the collective imagination was not an anomaly of modern politics but its inevitable corollary.

Anyone who wishes to understand the "historical" appearance of Yigal Amir, the student who assassinated Yitzhak Rabin (and the clandestine or overt groups who rallied to his political logic, if not his criminal act) must be able to decrypt the meaning of the borders of the national-territorial space in which this young "intellectual" murderer was raised and the distress occasioned by calling them into question. In the 1980s, primarily after the First Intifada and the international pressure on Israel, the political elite started to return portions of the "homeland territory" without sincerely trying to develop a new expression of the limits of the space of national existence. The traditional myth slowly weakened and retreated, but the liberal cultural elite did not assume the urgent critical responsibility of disarming the mythological mines planted in the Israeli political consciousness.

Amos Oz wrote his book *In the Land of Israel* after visiting the colony of Ofra, located in the heart of the "Land of Israel," with the aim of explaining to its inhabitants that their way was immoral and would lead to disaster. His unequivocal declaration that "we all agree without difficulty that the meaning of Zionism is that it is good for the Jewish people to return to the Land of Israel and bad for it to remain dispersed among the nations"[21] allowed him to open a dialogue with the colonists. At the time, this intellectual who dominated the Israeli Left, this sensitive writer, did not know that this statement, with all that it implies, caused him to lose the debate before it had even started. As long as Hebron and Nablus are considered to be "geographically" part of the "Land of Israel" like Jaffa or Haifa, those whose ethical scruples lead them to suggest retreat from the territories occupied since 1967 will be "caught" in a position of ideological inferiority.

The hegemony of mythological language in Israeli culture has blocked and continues to block the complete liberation from the specter of territorialism. Even as the importance of land loses its hold on most aspects of human life and practices, retreat from Judea and Samaria remains a problematic act casting a permanent shadow on the future of Israeli society. The danger of irredentism may continue to haunt the country's politics and there is the fear that the threat of new, unexpected "pogroms" will continue.

Praot Tarpat: The "Pogroms of the Year 5689"

Like the Jacobins of the French Revolution, Zionist intellectuals wanted a radical revolution in conceptions of time. Like the Jacobins, they tried, without much success, to break with the past ordered according to Christian chronology and to institute a new relationship with temporal periods. The secular Jacobins turned to a "rational and enlightened" future, while the Zionists, albeit secular as well, in order to escape the "exile mentality" that was a synonym of oppression, returned to the chronology of the pure Jewish religion. In each case, the universally accepted Christian notion of time put up resistance: use of the Hebrew calendar has remained marginal like a rear-guard fight; the debate is over. Western capitalism, which united the world in a single market economy, also forced it to agree to a homogenous and universal division of time that neither the walls of China nor five thousand years of Judaism could alter.

However, the choice of dating events according to the Hebrew calendar gives them an atemporal character that separates them from general history and participates in the creation of a national discourse that is distinct from the history of other peoples.

"Pogroms" also represent a distinct category. Using this term in reference to the first acts of violent resistance to Zionist colonization is an apparently deliberate reproduction of the Jewish *historia calamitatum*. The persistence of presenting the history of the Jews as a long chain of suffering and persecution culminated in the representation of "pogroms on the Land of Israel" the final stage and last gasps before national rebirth. The brutal and intolerant attitude of the indigenous inhabitants of Palestine towards those who had come to build their Jewish State "peacefully" and "calmly" is presented as another link in the chain of cruelty stretching back to the Kishinev pogrom.[22]

This approach assumes that human beings have always carried a hatred of Jews in their hearts and that they continue to pursue them even though they finally decided to return to their country that had remained empty, even if it had been temporarily inhabited by a local population (that unfortunately had no knowledge of the situation). The pioneering victims who claimed to own the country continued to represent themselves as a weak and persecuted minority even as they slowly but surely expanded their settlement territories and became a threat to their oldest neighbors due to territorial claims on the latter's living space. This self-image, which was formed at the same time as the earliest Jewish settlements, was no different in principle from the myths developed by other colonizing societies in modern history (anyone familiar with Hollywood westerns will easily recognize the image that the first pioneers projected of themselves).

The threat of "pogroms" and the propensity of the history of Zionist colonization to portray itself as a persecuted innocent have given Israeli society—the only one to possess nuclear weapons in the region—not only a constant justification in its own eyes, but also a well of deep-set collective anxieties that have influenced decision-making processes in the political arena. The history of the "pogroms" transmitted by school books and literature, but also projected onto the national conflict, contributed to the consolidation of a deterministic historical awareness where the security ideology of armed force fortified itself in a hegemonic position, completely out of proportion with the real relationships of force in the region. From Pharaoh to Haman the evil, from the Cossacks to Hitler, the "pogroms" of 1929 in Hebron formed the missing link in the collective imagination, the final piece in the logical historical unfolding leading to national rebirth.

It is of course possible to replace "pogroms of the year 5689" with "events of the year 5689." In place of the word "pogroms," many works use a more neutral term that, at first sight, seems free of any direct connotations to a specific subject or object. However, since the Arab revolt in 1936 and the general strike that followed were also called "events" we can detect in this linguistic choice a conscious ideological codification. This deliberate semantic neutralization aims to avoid expressions that could elicit a more precise understanding of Palestinian resistance to the colonization of the Jewish national movement.

Language, a Vector of Ideology?

Zionist colonization was not typical, even if the British domination of the region allowed it to become a historical reality. The Jewish national movement developed without the aid of a metropolitan country extending its power to overseas lands, exploiting its resources and sending its fleet or its army from time to time to put down the "indigenous" populations. However, its success was conditioned by appropriating a claimed territory where another human community lived. From this point of view, the consequences for the inhabitants in the long term were harsher than the destructive effects of classic colonialism[23]—it is difficult for Israeli intellectuals to accept this historical fact, especially those on the Left.

There is certainly a fundamental distinction between the colonization that took place before 1948 and the colonization that followed the 1967 War. In the first case, the colonists were mostly immigrants who had suffered from discrimination and persecution in their native countries, while in the second, they came from the territory of their national State where they enjoyed complete sovereignty. The victims of this colonization, however, see little difference between them. At first, they were asked to have consideration for the suffering of the Jews in Europe and then, in the following step, to pay the price for the "security needs" of the State of Israel. In each case, they continued to lose a little more control over their native land and their means of subsistence. "Settlement" and "colonization" are assumed to be synonyms, but each of these terms, in Hebrew, carries with it a different value judgment that determines the particular discourse on the reconstruction of local history. If we go back to the sentence describing the Hebrew national poet's journey in the 1920s (see above), it could have used words with a different significance as an introduction to a different history. For example: "Bialik left his country of origin and joined the fourth wave of the invasion of Palestine on the eve of the heroic insurrection of the Arab nation in 1929."

A similar turn of phrase could appear in an Arab school book: the ideological and didactic function resembles the "normative" Hebrew sentence that started this chapter. It would be fascinating to carry out a comparison between the categories of the political language of neighboring peoples who are opposed in national conflict, but such a comparison goes beyond the scope of my argument.[24]

Given the many choices available, one could also use a different formulation in Hebrew to transmit the "same" dry information about the great poet. For example: "Bialik left his native country and emigrated to the Palestinian Mandate before 1929, the year in which a series of riots and violent opposition to Zionist colonization erupted."

Israeli producers of culture, raised on the many linguistic mythologies that fill the Zionist historical imagination, still have difficulty expressing themselves in "unauthorized" terms like these. Is it necessary to add that these words are no more scientific and that it is illusory to believe they are neutral or represent a "happy medium"? Truth, contrary to the most widespread belief, is never found in the middle. It is always found where we least expect it, and we should never stop trying to uncover it.

Nevertheless, the last formulation of the sentence, unlike the preceding ones, attempts to deliver a somewhat more universal meaning. The attempt at universalism comes from any serious analysis of the situation in which we live that takes into account the understanding of the world by others. The sentence also includes some of the historical data previously mentioned: Bialik had difficulty leaving the land of his birth, his youth and his education. Immigration to the Middle East was a source of problems and struggle for him despite his adherence to the national project. During the 1920s, most people on the planet, including the Jews, Zionists and even the Hebraists, called the place in question "Palaestina," "Palestine" or "Falastin," especially since the majority of population in 1924 was comprised of Arab Palestinians and not the "Children of Israel." The bloody riot in 1929, as terrible and cruel as it was, was not a repetition of the pogroms that had taken place in Eastern Europe. It was one of the first phases of the long and deadly conflict over the processes of demographic change in the territory.

Human language is not only a tool for communication; it always transmits an ideology as well. The question remains as to the extent to which various linguistic elements serve as stumbling blocks in normalizing of our relationship to local history, in remembering others and in defining the rapidly changing collective identity of Israelis. Changing the words is not enough. The underlying politics and political culture must be changed.

However, the effort of questioning language to prevent it from thinking by itself through us, without control, should be one of the primary missions of intellectuals. Not only because they "think," as everyone does, but because they make their living, often quite well, from thinking.

3

"Analogical" Intellectuals

and the Gulf War

What then did they do to prevent it? What are they doing to put
an end to it? They are stirring up the bonfire, each one bringing
his faggot.
— Romain Rolland, *Above the Battle*, 1916. [trans. CK Ogden]

In every intellectual, even the most rational, there is an inspired
shaman always ready to be reborn.
— Edgar Morin, "Intellectuals: The Critique of Myth and the
Myth of Critique," 1961.

Soon after the end of fighting in the Gulf War in 1991, Dan
Miron, a well-known Israeli literary critic, explained how he had
his first reaction to the war while staying in the United States:

On the first day of the war, a Saturday, in New York, the television channel CNN broadcast a very long shot of Jerusalem,
where exactly nothing was happening. You could see an old
Jewish man starting out to morning prayer on the Sabbath.
Wearing a kippah and a fur hat, he moved quickly in the

deserted street. The camera's close up accentuated the features of his face marked by sweat and fear as a siren rang out. The poor Jew continued on with hesitant strides, filmed for almost three minutes, which on television seems like an eternity.[1]

This scene provoked Dan Miron's anger. A supporter of the Left and undoubtedly one of the leading Israeli intellectuals, he expressed one of the harshest critiques in the Israeli cultural domain of his country's non-intervention in the war. In February 1991, he published an article with the title, "If there is Tzahal, let it show itself at once!" paraphrasing a line by the poet Hayim Nahman Bialik who had exclaimed during the Kichniev pogrom of the early 20th century:

> "If there is justice, let it show itself at once!" Unlike Bialik, Miron knew that justice often needs force to be enacted. And living in a country where the use of force is frequent, it seemed natural to him to demand that his government send troops against the threat of a new "pogrom."[2]

His fiery stance is not representative of the reactions in Israeli cultural spheres to the conflict. While the large majority of Israeli intellectuals stated their support of the war without reservation and often with enthusiasm, they also accepted the decision of the Israeli government, after pressure from the Americans, to abstain from any direct intervention into the conflict.

This chapter will examine how Israeli intellectuals reacted to the Gulf War in light of the changes that have affected the status of "major intellectuals" and the ways that they intervene in a Western culture dominated by electronic and audiovisual media.

Intellectuals and Analogical Memory

The advent of liberal democracy at the end of the 19th century helped give the intellectual elite a relatively autonomous power in relation to State power. We must also note that this autonomous power encountered the press's claim to bring the truth to the masses. In the Dreyfus Affair, for example, one part of the new intellectual elite was not content to question political and military power but also appeared as a movement against accepted wisdom and the prejudices conveyed in the press about the accused starting in 1895.

The struggle in 1898 to win public opinion assumed the dimensions of a confrontation between two different levels of knowledge producers and moral imperatives: against the general press, which had shaped public opinion for three years, the intellectuals mobilized as producers of deep symbols and made use of the new vectors of communication to align the cultural sphere with the direction of their political and moral vision. Since then, and not only in France, liberal democracy confirmed the idea of greater autonomy for intellectuals and even revealed itself to be tolerant of their incursions into the political arena. With the start of the era of parliamentary democracy, where discourse participates in the regulation of relationships between political forces, a leading role was left to the masters of words, the intellectuals.

However, as we know, changes in the means of production led to changes in the relationships of production; these changes also reached the production and diffusion of knowledge. At the end of the 19th century, producers of high culture, using their mastery of the word, were able to have some hold over the "duplicators" and distributors of culture. In a civilization where visual media have become the primary location of the production of knowledge, however, the status of the "duplicators" of culture has been strengthened at the expense of the producers.

While the "major intellectuals" coming from universities and laboratories have had success in entering the world of the press, the same is not true of television studios, where the producers of written culture have had to abandon their dominant position, with a few rare exceptions. As images have replaced writing, classic intellectuals have witnessed the collapse of part of the symbolic moral capital they had accumulated since the formation of the democratic public arena.

The Gulf War marked a key event in the modification of this relationship of cultural forces. We could witness a sophisticated coordination between Western political powers and electronic communications networks that produced an impressive audiovisual representation while simultaneously providing the flow and the filter of information as well as the immediate moral framework that emerged from it.

From the start, the images shown on CNN established very clearly who was good and who was bad, who the attacker was and who the victim was. The pictures of the old Jewish man in the street were followed by Scuds fired at night, then babies assassinated in Kuwait by Iraqi soldiers—later revealed to be a montage. The tens of thousands of victims in Iraq were never shown on screen: the two protagonists of the war found a common interest.

What could intellectuals of the elite add to this daily mass of audiovisual images? Jean-Luc Godard said in one of his films that "cinema is the truth twenty-four times per second." The live television rebroadcasts work to convince us of the truth of this expression. Can there be a truth truer than this "living reality" that we watch at the very moment that it is taking place?

This "living reality" creates the profound awareness of a transparent, directly comprehensible reality that has no need of conceptualization. The feeling of being a direct witness of real events reduces the status of major intellectuals who are (were?) the traditional mediators of culture. This new "information and communications" culture is bound to develop the ethos of intellectuals involved in revealing hidden truths (the idea originating in the Dreyfus affair). From there to conclude the absolute uselessness of intellectual elites is a giant leap. During dramatic events, in times of crisis, the capital accumulated by intellectual elite, even devalued capital, remains useful in the political arena.

A study of the forms of intervention and positions taken by Israeli intellectuals during the Gulf War shows that the essential cultural role, although not the only one, left to "major" producers of culture was drawing historical parallels. Intellectuals tried to decrypt a confused reality; they were like agents who define an ethics of political data and create or refute social and political symbols. But does the public really need this kind of spiritual assistance today? This function seems to be become more and more superfluous and the preference is now given to people who perpetuate a "heritage," who contribute to the collective consciousness by creating analogies, and primarily historical analogies.

Of course, televised images are already full of objects of comparison—for example, the frightened old Jewish man in Jerusalem. Audiovisual journalists, like those in the press, constantly replaced the Gulf War in a historical context where it was easy to distinguish the good guys and the bad guys.

No political thought could exist without analogies. Translating associative analogies into consistent and specific conceptual analogies, however, remains the prerogative of "major" intellectuals.

While they discover the present projected on television screens at the same time as their contemporaries, they have a greater knowledge of the past and may therefore be more ready to imagine the future.

In order to flesh out the idea that, in times of crisis, intellectuals make an analogical contribution to political concepts, I will take examples from the production of Israeli academics, writers and artists whose intellectual production was not blighted by Scuds. The quotes, some of which are deliberately extensive, all come from the print media. No examples were taken from audiovisual materials, despite their interest, due to the difficulty of quoting them. Given the limited scope of this chapter, only renowned intellectuals who are recognized leaders in their domains and, in political terms, on the Left, which retains cultural hegemony despite the political upheaval of 1977.

Most "ranking" intellectuals adopted positions that were identical to those of the "leading" intellectuals, including the support for military action against Iraq. Only a few isolated individuals expressed reserves about single-minded approval of warmongering logic. A further illustration of the fact that in times of crisis and when facing an external enemy, intellectuals are not as divided as in times of internal political discord.

Academics and Evil Tyrants

For analogies with the past, it is best to begin with those who are responsible for maintaining collective memory: historians. Since the passing of Yaacov Talmon, the eminent historian who would write sweeping, programmatic articles in the press during a crisis, no figure of equal stature has appeared in Israel. But there is no lack of historians producing scientific analogies.

In January 1991, after hanging a large Israeli flag from his balcony and calling on all of his fellow citizens to do the same, Michael Harsgor, of the University of Tel Aviv, was interviewed for a leftist newspaper.[3] Claiming to be a "specialist of oligarchies, tyrants, dictators and other absolute powers," Harsgor declared that he had reached the conclusion that Saddam Hussein represented a typical case of the megalomania found throughout history. He cited Philippe II of Spain, Benito Mussolini, Gamal Abdel Nasser and of course Adolf Hitler. How did Saddam Hussein resemble Philippe II? The Spanish sovereign looked down on the technological superiority of the Anglo-Dutch coalition confronting him, an attitude that resembled the position of the Iraqi dictator on the Western coalition. How did he resemble Mussolini? Like the latter, he sought advice from magicians and astrologists. And like Nasser, Saddam Hussein was the product of Muslim fanaticism caused by the underdevelopment of Arab countries: "There are clocks in churches. Has anyone ever seen a clock in a mosque?"

The shadow of Adolf Hitler, the supreme demon, loomed the largest in the interview. Michael Harsgor found in Saddam Hussein "significant similarities with the irrational murderous fanaticism of Hitler." He added,

> the propensity for creating imaginary enemies is also strong in Saddam. What do we [Israel] have to do with the conflict in Kuwait? Saddam has made us his enemy for internal political needs, which makes him undoubtedly like Hitler. For me, he is capable of doing everything Hitler did.

Michael Harsgor, who is an experienced historian, seemed to have forgotten that a few years earlier Israel, the only nuclear power in the Middle East, bombed and destroyed the Osirak nuclear reactor in Iraq! Nevertheless, in order to make the historical parallels more striking, he also drew on personal memories:

> He [Saddam Hussein] is very much like Hitler in another way. He does not know how to stay quiet. When Hitler entered the Rhineland, France could have swept him out with 10,000 soldiers. Yet when my father made the remark to our French neighbor, he replied, "Monsieur, we will not go to war for people like you, for the Jews."

Comparing Saddam Hussein to Hitler was nothing new or original to Harsgor. The American president at the time, George Bush Sr., had established the analogy before the war began and, as we will see, it is omnipresent among Israeli intellectuals (and many intellectuals in Europe and the United States). Harsgor, however, added a further dimension: he expressed his fear of pacifists rushing to Saddam's aid and compared them to the Anti-Semitic pacifists in France on the eve of the Second World War.

The theme of "dangerous" pacifism was amply mentioned by Moshe Zimmermann, professor of history at the Hebrew University of Jerusalem and specialist in contemporary Germany. In February 1991, he published an important article under the title "Deadly Pacifism."[4] Why "deadly"? Because, "without the pacifist demonstrations, Saddam might have decided that the West was ready for war and would have acted differently."

How can the truth of this statement be proven when the historian has so little information about the decision-making process inside the Iraqi dictatorship, unless he is using an analogy? Zimmermann quotes a German politician from the 1980s who declared: "pacifism led to Auschwitz." The statement came in an attack against pacifists opposed to the installation of Pershing missiles. In the same way, Moshe Zimmermann suggested the hypothesis that "if the pacifist movement had won, the chances of the collapse of Communist regimes would have been much weaker." Yet the pacifism of the 1980s, which opposed the arms race of the Cold War, may not have been the best historical lesson, especially since the lessons of history are soon forgotten. According to Zimmermann:

> There is a lesson that we may have retained, also from German history: when Hitler came to power, students at Oxford swore an oath to prevent Great Britain from entering a war. Hitler took notice and when he sent his troops to the left bank of the Rhine, which was supposed to remain demilitarized, neither France nor Great Britain reacted. European pacifism also forced inaction when German troops entered Austria and then Czechoslovakia. In other words, the country without a pacifist movement took advantage of the pacific ideals of its adversaries to conquer and oppress.

The historian called on the reactions of these Oxford students, so closely watched by Hitler, along with the leaders of France and Great Britain on the eve of the Second World War to make a historical comparison with those who opposed the Gulf War, who questioned the politics of their governments. Zimmermann hoped that the analogy he built would have a greater echo with readers who may have heard of Chamberlain or Daladier but knew nothing about the "murderous" students of Oxford.

Shlomo Avineri is a reputed political scientist teaching at the Hebrew University of Jerusalem; he is considered to be one of the leading Marx and Hegel specialists in the world and often has more of a historian's approach than many historians. He also gave his interpretation of the war in February 1991 by publishing a long, sophisticated article, moderate in tone, where he expressed the idea that Middle Eastern oil could not continue to be dominated by reactionary Arab leaders nor continue to be the sole property of Arab peoples.[5] Just as the end of the Second World War saw the creation of the UN, the Gulf War should end in a new type of internationalization: reform of the national idea of appropriation of natural resources, making oil the property of the international community. It seems, however, that Shlomo Avineri's generous proposal did not include the wells in Texas or the North Sea!

In reaching his radical conclusion, the political scientist offered his own historical parallels for the conflict, using analogies to understand the personality of Saddam Hussein.

> There is a resemblance between him and Hitler; and I do not use the comparison for propaganda as many Westerners (and Israelis) have done, but I want to provide an objective basis. Hitler was able to gain the sympathy of such a large part of the German public in the early 1930s because Germany had many justifiable grievances against Western countries after the First World War and the Treaty of Versailles [...]. In the same way, Saddam uses the feelings of justified anger and frustration in the Arab world.[6]

Shlomo Avineri knew perfectly well that his readers would feel no empathy towards the "justified grievances" of the Germans, precisely because of Hitler; therefore, using an analogy of this type could only lead to relativizing the "feelings of justified anger and frustration" of Arab peoples towards the oil monarchies left behind by colonialism in the Middle East.

Hitler and the world of 1939–1945 guided Shlomo Avineri's entire analysis and, for him, the "parallels with Saddam Hussein are stunning." He insisted on the following historical conclusion:

> By provoking the entire world, Saddam Hussein ensured himself an end that resembles Hitler's. The allied forces may not yet be aware of it, but war with Saddam will have to be a total war in order to be victorious.[7]

Unlike Michael Harsgor and Moshe Zimmermann, Shlomo Avineri did not attack the pacifism of the 1980s and did not succumb to the temptation of assimilating it with the pacifism of the 1930s. Yet the support given by the Western world to Iraq in its struggle against Muslim fundamentalism sparked another memory of the period:

> Historians will remember that an alignment of circumstances of this kind had already tempted the West in the 1930s, and its indulgence towards Hitler came in part from the fact that he was seen as an effective barrier against communism, which led many to close their eyes on the criminal aspects of Nazism.[8]

Writers and Good Wars

Academics were not the only ones to criticize the conciliatory and pacifist tendencies in Europe; some of the most famous Israeli writers joined them. Starting on January 28, 1991, several authors and poets, including Amos Oz, A.B. Yehoshua and Yoram Kaniuk, held a press conference in Tel Aviv during which they strenuously condemned the pacifist rallies being held in the Western world.[9] "War is not the worst thing a society can experience," declared Amos Oz, adding that he was "a man of peace but not a pacifist" and that everyone knew that the Jews had received expressions of sympathy "after the Holocaust and after the threats of extermination in 1967, and still now. Maybe in the Western mind our place is on the cross?" According to Oz, the time for playing the victim in history was over; it was time to support the coalition and the war. The fall of Saddam Hussein's regime was a precondition for the return of the peace process. Asked about the possible use of nuclear weapons by Israel, Amos Oz replied:

> If the choice is between that and a second Auschwitz, then there is no choice. Generally speaking, however, I am against the use of this type of weapon.

A.B. Yehoshua also criticized the pacifists and called for what he named "Saddam Hussein's war machine" to be crushed. Yet when pushed by a foreign journalist who was questioning him about protests in Germany, he responded with a certain amount of condescension: "You know, I do not oppose any protest in Germany against the war. It is better for Germans to rally for peace for a century and let others wage war...."

Yoram Kaniuk, one of the intellectuals who is the most involved in the struggle for Palestinian rights, engaged in a public confession where he told how an Arab writer had contacted him to persuade him not to participate in the press conference or to attack the pacifist movement. Kaniuk replied with a question: "What would you have said to writers during Hitler's time?"

The press conference by Israeli intellectuals was extensively covered by the media and the participants followed it in different ways: Amoz Oz gave a long interview to newspaper journalists and Yoram Kaniuk was invited to Germany to express his antipacifist positions more effectively.

Amos Oz, at the beginning of his interview "There are Just Wars," revealed his model for comparison:

> I cannot help thinking that if the position of the German pacifists today had prevailed throughout the world in 1939, neither you nor I [speaking to the journalist] would be alive here. There were very evil people in power at the time.[10]

Of course, Amos Oz continued to proclaim his support for peace and for compromise with the Palestinians, even though they supported Saddam Hussein and, according to him, their national movement was "one of the most hideous of the modern era." It would be interesting to know to whom or to what he was comparing them: Zionism, the Ustaše, the Mau Mau in Kenya, the Algerian FLN, the Vietcong, the Khmer Rouge? For the writer, it was lucky that the Zionist Left built the Dimona[11] nuclear reactor and that Israel had an aeronautics industry. He finally admitted that he should not have attacked Menachem Begin when he took the wise decision to bomb the nuclear reactor in Iraq.

The journalist shows great interest in Amos Oz's conception of history and asks him: "Tolstoy claimed that individuals, no matter how great, cannot determine the course of history." How did the writer respond? He indicated his line of thinking:

> I am a great admirer of Tolstoy's conception of history, which states that farmers will determine the order of things; but I am not sure that things happen that way. Churchill wrote in his memoirs that his primary mistake, in the Second World War, was not to have ordered the physical elimination of Hitler [...]. It is true that if, God forbid, John Major were assassinated, the fate of the world would not change, not even Great Britain's position on the Gulf War. The same would probably be true of George Bush. However, I am not sure that the same is true of Saddam Hussein [...]. The weight of a personality in history changes depending on the circumstances. Russia would be very different if Stalin had died young [...]. Stalin put his mark on the country, including his madness and trauma, to say nothing of Germany [...].

Yoram Kaniuk, for his part, spoke a great deal about Germany and the Gulf War. In an article titled "Three and a Half Hours and Fifty Years with Günter Grass in Berlin," he spoke of the "cock fight" he had with the author of *The Tin Drum* on German television.[12] The two men had met before the Gulf War and complimented each other at the start of their televised exchange; the Israeli writer, however, warned his readers:

> After twenty minutes, the child who had joined the Hitlerjugend, the young man who had shot at low-flying American

planes came out and the skin drum became a kind of steel drum. I had come for a dialog and the Israeli-Palestinian Committee and my more than thirty-year quest for peace. Everything vanished and we were left with nothing. I was my grandfather and he was his; the German against the Jew.

The strong feeling of a resurgence of the past seized Yoram Kaniuk when Günter Grass, the great destroyer of Nazism and more generally of German nationalism, declared that he did not accept the reasoning behind the historical comparison between "what happened in Israel and German gas." The Nobel Prize winner refused to admit that entering into hermetically sealed rooms was, for Israelis, the equivalent of a return to the Warsaw ghetto. Despite his support for using Patriot missiles to destroy Scuds and save human lives, the German writer opposed providing new submarines to Israel. Yoram Kaniuk, upset, could only explain this "surprising" political attitude by calling on the personal history of the young Günter Grass, always and forever entwined with that of his German parents, grandparents and great-grandparents.

The writer Yitzhak Orpaz, a very incisive novelist, used the same historical logic to explain the German position:

> The grandfather made Zyklon-B, the son made Saddam's chemical weapons and the grandson, in the name of pacifism and the Left, rallied for the Iraqi führer.[13]

Another talented writer, Haim Beer, went even further, saying that leftist intellectuals in Germany were simply "revealing the Nazi genes of their fathers."[14]

Artists and Important Guests

Inserting biology into history was not limited to academics and writers. The Gulf War also elicited reactions and further analogies from Israeli artists. Yigal Tomarkin, renowned sculptor and leftist, composed an open letter to his friends in the European pacifist Left who were protesting against the war:

> Your parents sprayed Zyklon-B in public showers (as they were called, since the dirty Jews had to bathe), the best of them merely denounced or suddenly turned away from their neighbors of the day before. Be they from Germany, France, Poland or elsewhere, I know that the just among them never forgave us for crucifying Jesus.[15]

Tomarkin's anger towards the descendants of these assassins and snitches is not only fueled by the eternal damnation of their parents, but also by the fact that instead of Israel they prefer underdeveloped and fanatic Arabs, the descendants of the desert who despite their black goats have always lived as parasites, destroying every culture in their path. How could they not understand that "the fall of Israel will signal the fall of the West"? The sculptor concludes: "It seems that, like their fathers, they have an active anti-Jewish gene...."

I could continue to list a long string of "analogical" pearls dropped by important Israeli intellectuals; we would find both crude and subtle expressions. The picture would not be complete if we left out the original contributions of two non-Israeli intellectuals who came to Jerusalem during the War and during their public appearances they participated in expressing the heightened imagination of a shell-shocked society.

Elie Wiesel, writer of the Shoah, who was staying at the King David Hotel in Jerusalem, put on a gas mask during the Scud alerts and gave his immediate impressions to an Israeli journalist:

> "Putting on this gas mask, I had the feeling of going backwards; civilization was going backwards, humanity was going backwards, history was going backwards."[16] And to another paper: "It was a terrifying spectacle, indescribable! Imagine children, little children, wearing masks to protect themselves from gas made by Germans."[17]

Moved by some intellectual obligation, he added a few words on pacifists in the world:

> Why don't they organize popular rallies, why don't they collect petitions signed by famous names to protest the criminal use of gas against the Jewish citizens of a country like Israel, which is not taking part in the combat?

The writer confused reality and imagination: very fortunately, there was no "German" gas. The Nobel Prize winner quickly felt confined in Israel and left for New York, leaving his place to another specialist of the Shoah, Claude Lanzmann. He was also quick to don a gas mask and immediately confided: "I have the impression of being back in 1940 when all the borders in Europe were closed...."[18]

Presumably his film on the Israeli army encouraged Claude Lanzmann to take on the role of military advisor: "If there is a gas attack, Iraq should be bombarded with tactical atomic weapons." After accusing Israeli authorities of not understanding the real motivations of Saddam Hussein (for him, the war was aimed at Israel from the start, and the Jews were threatened with extermination), Lanzmann did not hesitate to compare Israeli leaders to the members of the Judenräte who did not understand the objectives of their exterminators during the Holocaust.

Specificity of the Executioner or the Victim

Intellectuals from a wide variety of professional fields led the charge of comparative imagination. As we have seen, from the megalomania of Philippe II, foolish enough to fight Shakespeare's England, to the Judenräte, including the Kichniev pogrom, Israel had to face the Scuds and digest the historical imagination of its intellectuals. It seems that like the Scuds, these comparisons did not contribute to reinforcing the country's feelings of security or the lucidity of their readers. This imaginary, with its repertory of models, only heightened the Manichean vision of the world produced by the audiovisual media. Images are not enough; the world still needs words, and in particular words that can create reference points.

Making analogies between present and past events is a perfectly legitimate approach. Instrumentalizing the past to understand better what is happening in the present is part of human experience. Every historian knows that there is no "pure" collective memory; public memory is always turned towards the needs of the time. Moreover, it is certain that preserving the memory of the defeated is a duty that reflects the morality of any modern civilization, but we cannot in this case refrain from adding that the victims of yesterday can become the conquerors of tomorrow.

The thoughts of a large majority of Israeli (and Jewish) intellectuals focused on Hitler, the Second World War and the Shoah during the Gulf War. Considering the tragic fate of the Jews during the first half of the 20th century, indulgence for these historical references might be understood. However, isn't there a permanent refusal in Israeli culture to compare the Jewish Holocaust to any other historical event? When any scholar who hazards a comparison between the genocide of the Jews and that of the gypsies or the Armenians is seen as desecrating the memory of the Jewish victims, the speed with which any enemy of the State of Israel is turned into Hitler is hard to believe, and to stomach.

In defending the unique character of the Shoah, very few Israeli intellectuals base their argument on the specificity of Nazism and its unprecedented project of industrial murder. The specificity of the victims comes first—the suffering of the Jews could never be compared to the victims of any other genocide. That is why, for example, Elie Wiesel and several Israeli historians left a conference on the extermination of peoples to which Armenian speakers had been invited.[19] And it is why Nasser was once called the Arab Hitler, why Arafat was compared to Hitler and why, during the Gulf War, a strong intellectual consensus formed around describing the Iraqi leader as a new Hitler.

In truth, despite this vast consensus, some marginal voices of protest could be heard. The camp of critical intellectuals who opposed the war before it started fell apart and fell silent when the first Scud was launched. Some returned to their previous pacifist position. A few young journalists mocked the truckloads of historical analogies dumped by "major" intellectuals, but the avalanche of knowledge issuing from the literary elite and university chairs made them more hesitant.

There were, nonetheless, two figures from the "high" Israeli intelligentsia who dared speak openly about their reservations concerning the justification of the war and who deliberately refrained from joining the cult of historical analogies surrounding them. Yeshayahu Leibowitz, professor at the Hebrew University of Jerusalem, and Mattityahu Peled, a former general of the Israeli Army who had become a professor of Arab Literature at the University of Tel Aviv, refused to see this conflict as a struggle between the forces of light and darkness.[20] The results of the 1967 War had already led these two thinkers into a process of increasing refusal of the dominant logic in Israeli political culture in all parties. They publically opposed Israel's war in Lebanon in 1982 from the start, without waiting for its strategic and moral failures to become apparent, unlike others.

Other Israeli intellectuals probably understood that the smell of oil today should not be confused with yesterday's smell of gas and that a cynical war by raiders seeking energy and raw materials could not be turned into a war to defend innocent victims even through the magic of verbal analogies. Yet the shock of the Scuds— their echo could be heard in the coastal regions of Israel—did not allow this minority, including myself, to display their intellectual courage. Yeshayahu Leibowitz, with his university prestige and religious faith, and Mattityahu Peled, with his security experience prior to academia, were the only ones who could allow themselves to go beyond the representation of Jews as eternal victims.

In conclusion, I must ask my readers not to dwell too long on the quote from Romain Rolland at the beginning of this chapter. The quotation can be explained by the fact that I have my own repertoire of historical models that help me think the present. Proving, once again, how hard it is to be an agent of verbal culture without producing analogies.

4

Post-Zionism: A Historiographical

or Intellectual Debate?

Forgetting, I would even go so far as to say historical error, is a crucial factor in the creation of a nation, which is why progress in historical studies often constitutes a danger for [the principle of] nationality.
— Ernest Renan, "What Is a Nation?," 1882.

The problem is not one of changing people's "consciousness" or what's in their heads; but the political, economic, institutional regime of the production of truth.
— Michel Foucault, "The Political Function of the Intellectual," 1976.

At the end of the year 1987, the Palestinian insurrection erupted in the occupied territories, better known to the public in its Arab name as the Intifada. It marked a turn in the development of the Israeli historical consciousness. In the same year, Simha Flapan published *The Birth of Israel: Myths and Realities*, and a year later, in the thick of the conflict, three more studies appeared on similar topics: *Collusion Across the Jordan: King Abdullah, the Zionist*

Movement and the Partition of Palestine, by Avi Shlaim, *Britain and the Arab-Israeli Conflict, 1948–1951*, by Ilan Pappé; and *The Birth of the Palestinian Refugee Problem, 1947–1949*, by Benny Morris. In 1988, Boaz Evron open a wide field of thinking by publishing *A National Reckoning*, and in the following year Gershon Shafir's socio-historical study was published, *Land, Labor and the Origins of the Israeli Palestinian Conflict, 1882–1914*.[1]

In fact, studies calling into question the central theses of Zionist historiography had been published before but were still only isolated and sporadic cases. Relegated to the margins of political and intellectual (and rarely university) fields, they remained without follow-up or failed to generate significant echoes.[2] At the end of the 1980s, however, the polemic on the nature of Zionism and Israel's politics took hold in journals and conferences and spilled into the pages of the daily newspapers, and even began to receive some attention from the audiovisual media and entered some high school textbooks. Soon after the signing of the Oslo Accords in 1993, this trend, known globally as "post-Zionism," began to be recognized as a possible way to rethink the history of Zionism and the State of Israel, even though it was far from being adopted as the primary and hegemonic interpretation.

The national and international diffusion of this innovative writing, as well as the interest and the controversy surrounding some of them in the media, are probably connected to the dynamic created by the Palestinian insurrection and its impact on the evolution of thinking. It is not possible, however, to establish a cause and effect relationship between the confrontations and the birth of this new historiographical approach. While the Palestinian revolt was characterized by its spontaneity, these studies had been undertaken long before their publication, some as doctoral theses. They cannot, therefore, be seen as the direct product of unfolding events. The explanation for the curious simultaneity between these two phenomena may be found in historical processes that had begun to unfold ten years before, long before they became public.

Before entering the heart of the subject and separating the causes of this historiographical evolution on the one hand and its theoretical content on the other, we must reconstruct the institutional context in which these studies took shape, as well as the characteristics and models of power relationships into which they entered. We should recall that outside Boaz Evron's book in Hebrew, all of the aforementioned works were published in Britain or the United States and some of them never appeared in Israel. Moreover, despite the fact that the authors were all Israeli, none of them was a member of a Jewish history department in an Israeli university. According to the professional criteria of Israeli historiography, none of them fit the profile of an "accredited" historian in their field of specialization. To further understand this institutional aspect, we must go back to another historical period.

Institutions

In 1936, the year of the Palestinian "Great Revolt," the Hebrew University of Jerusalem, founded ten years before, opened its first History department. Notwithstanding the initial project, two entirely distinct departments were created: one dedicated to teaching Jewish history and the other to general history. Since Jewish philosophy had already received its own department—it was separated from the structure for teaching general philosophy—the decision raised little protest and was even welcomed by the historians, who had first opposed it. The reasons for this separation were in part connected to power struggles within the university, but they were primarily driven by the national conception that most instructors at the new university shared: from the point of view of the Zionist revolution, it was important to avoid "blurring the boundaries" between the history of the "Jewish nation" conceived of as a "living organism" and universal history that might "swallow" it![3] The symbiosis between religious-traditionalist exclusivity and national necessity tipped the balance in favor of the creation of a specifically Jewish historiography.

In all Western cultures, starting at the end of the 19th century, historiography contributed to the construction of national identity, but there were few cases where national history was separated in such a structural and categorical way from the history of other nations. The principle of universality inherent in the way history is taught in Europe, with all of the contradictions and affectation that have always accompanied it, was not adopted by the founders of the first history department created in Jerusalem. Not without irony, since two years after the declaration of the Nuremburg Laws, the Jewish history taught at the Hebrew University turned into a compartmentalized discipline, an isolated one, despite all historical logic, from the history of "normal" human societies.

As soon as it was institutionalized, this new discipline produced unique concepts that were unknown to the domain of general history. The concept forged in the mid-19th century in both Jewish historiography and Zionist thought that for two thousand years Jews had formed an ethnic nation in political exile striving for a return to their original homeland was validated by university authority to the point of being seen as a scientific truth and inspired academic research and publications. It is remarkable that Zionist thought retranscribed into the modern national duality "exile/homeland" the religious and metaphysical contradiction nestled at the heart of Jewish belief in the concepts of "exile/redemption." The Zionist historiography developed in Jerusalem turned this new principle of contradiction into a guiding principle, both in the reconstruction of Jewish communities and in the definition of their way to refer to the Holy Land. The Jewish past therefore gained a unique resonance, making it irreconcilable with the past of other religious civilizations in the pre-modern world. Yitzhak Baer, the first professional historian of the history of the Jews at the Hebrew University of Jerusalem, expressed the character of this historiographical tendency, affirming that "a force exists that lifts the Jewish people above the contingencies of causal history."[4] In the same spirit, research dedicated to the Zionist undertaking rejected any analogy with the development of other national or colonizing societies in modern times: the Zionists had not emigrated to Palestine or colonized it. They "rose" and returned to their home after two thousand years of wandering; and the supreme proof of their ownership rights over the land is written in the Book of books.

The teachings of the Bible, used more as a book of national history than as sacred religious canons, also became a separate subject in primary and secondary education in the eyes of the first immigrant community in Palestine. Each student in every level of the Hebrew school system studies the history of their collective past separately from universal history. It was logical that the development of the collective memory was completed by an adequate university education. The "three-thousand year-old Jewish nation" had the right to a separate field of pedagogy and research prohibited to "unaccredited" historians who would presume to access it. One of the most striking results of this original approach was that from the 1930s to the 1990s, no teacher or researcher from the various departments of "History of the Jewish People" in Israeli universities considered him- or herself to be a non-Zionist historian. Historians of general history whose Zionist identity was not always as confirmed had the freedom to treat questions dealing with Jewish history, but they were ineligible for budgets, scholarships, research institutes, chairs or directing doctoral theses related to Jewish history. To complete the picture, we should add that Middle Eastern history quickly received its own department and, to this day, this division of the past into three domains—general history, Jewish history and Middle Eastern history—is found in all Israeli universities. A Jewish history student can pass three degrees without learning anything about general history. And a general or Middle Eastern history student is not required to take any classes in Jewish or Israeli history.[5]

Under these conditions, it is not surprising that the historiographical turn that began at the end of the 1980s was started by "outsiders." Simha Flapan and Boaz Evron, the oldest of this group of new scholars, did not belong to university circles and corresponded to the definition of "amateur historians." Talented essayists embodying the image of the leftist intellectual, they pursued their research for years without financial aid or any support from official institutions. The four other scholars mentioned above, all a generation younger, finished their studies abroad. Ilan Pappé and Benny Morris obtained positions in Israeli universities after publishing their work, but they did not join one of the "History of the Jewish People" departments. Avi Shlaim and Gershon Shafir teach in Britain and the United States respectively, and their work, like that of Ilan Pappé, has not been translated into Hebrew. None of the Israeli scholars who have joined the contestation of conventions in research on the past followed the normal curriculum of Jewish historiography. Some, like Baruch Kimmerling, Uri Ram, Uri Ben Eliezer and Yehuda Shenav, come from a sociology background; others specialized in Middle Eastern studies; still others studied political science or linguistics. Journalists, writers and poets later came to join their ranks.

There is a series of causes that directly or indirectly helped create a favorable climate for this unprecedented contestation at the end of the 1980s. We should start with the impact of structural changes: the slow changes in the way of life and standard of living following the rise in GNP, the reduction of state control over cultural production in parallel with the increase in institutions and actors in this sector modified the structures through which the collective memory was formed. The proliferation of audiovisual means of communication heightened the symbiosis between national culture and American-style cultural "globalization." At the end of the 1970s, the convergence of these two factors contributed to forming a different liberal sensibility in both cultural and political domains.[6]

The start of this intellectual turning point can be found in a political event that best reflected long term changes. The 1977 elections that brought Menachem Begin and his political party, the Likud, to power, alienated of a large sector of the Israeli intelligentsia with the new regime of the Zionist Right. From the 1930s until then, an ideological alliance had been maintained between the dominant political and intellectual elite. The myths and ethics of socialist Zionism had cemented the ties between the intellectual class and the all-powerful political center, leaving aside only a few marginal cases with no impact on cultural or university life. After 1977, however, intellectuals, including their most prominent figures, did not hesitate to express their discontent with the government of the new ruling class that had sometimes rejected the intellectuals with disdain. The antagonistic relationship reinforced political neo-liberalism in Israel, to which the growth in the means of production and cultural distribution had already contributed.

Signing the peace treaty with Egypt did not quell the intellectual revolt against power. One might even think that it helped consolidate or create the conditions for developing critiques and contestation, because the siege mentality that had characterized Israeli culture until that time significantly diminished. In 1982, the Lebanon War waged by the Right against the Palestinian people heightened the alienation of the intellectual elite with the government, be it neo-liberal or, even more so, from the political Left. The new generation led the protests, the generation that had not lived through the "national rebirth" of 1948 and did not feel bound by the past or obliged to hold it in reverence. Critical works first began to appear in literature and film at the start of the 1980s, questioning the relationship of Israelis with their past and with the space where it took place.

The development of relationships between the political sphere and intellectual circles, complicated by the growing tension between generations, proved conducive to new historical thinking and especially to its "reception." Yet it was another circumstantial factor that allowed some of this new research to begin. After 30 years, government archives were opened to the public: documents relating to the British withdrawal and the ensuing war in 1948 became accessible. The work of Benny Morris, Ilan Pappé and Avi Shlaim, to name only a few, used the newly accessible information gathered in these files. The basic hypotheses, assumptions and arguments concerning the creation of the State of Israel, which were an integral part of the rhetoric of the non-Zionist, and in some cases Zionist, Left, but were particularly defended by Palestinian scholars, could finally be verified with the archives, forcing traditional historians to respond.

The new climate of theoretical debate in the West—and in particular in the Anglo-Saxon world where the national question was studied using new conceptual approaches—encouraged the critical audacity of some scholars. While the influence of Benedict Anderson, Ernest Gellner or Eric Hobsbawm, for example, remained light in the first critical essays of the new Israeli historians, their working hypotheses later occupied the center of the debate.[7] Ideas inspired by British thought penetrated Israeli intellectual and university circles along with the changing identity approaches from the West and they also contributed to the first reservations expressed about official Israeli historiography.[8] The historiographical controversy involved four main points:

1. the circumstances of the 1948 War and its consequences;

2. the positions and actions of the Zionist movement and governments towards the Shoah and its victims as well as immigration from Muslim countries;

3. the characteristics of Zionist colonization since the end of the 19th century;

4. the perception of the Jewish past as national history. What debates did these topics create, what were their scope and their limits?

The 1948 War

It is not by chance that the first critiques took the 1948 War for their object. The books of official history presented this conflict as a just and heroic struggle for national sovereignty, then, after the attack by the Arab countries, as a defensive war by a minority engaged in a combat for survival. However, and surprising as it may seem, the founding event of the State of Israel was not the object of any serious research until the 1980s. The previous work that had been dedicated to it was mainly apologetic. It relied on written and oral memories, and on press reports of the time. Access to the closed archives was strictly reserved to "trustworthy" historians—some of whom had occupied positions in the military—who knew how to control and censure themselves.

Simha Flapan drew primarily at the source of official publications; he had distinguished himself by using the personal diaries of Ben-Gurion and documents from State public archives. Despite being an avowed Zionist,[9] he launched a severe critique of the foundation myth of the 1948 War that fed the Israeli collective memory. According to his conclusions, the Jewish leadership did not accept the partition of Mandate Palestine and the secret accord concluded in 1947 with Abdullah, the King of Jordan, was part of a global strategy to prevent the creation of a Palestinian State. During the war, the exodus of refugees was encouraged by the Israeli political and military administration. Flapan also questioned the relationship of forces between Israel and Arab countries, opposing a weak Jewish minority against a strong Arab majority. But mostly his demonstration showed how the Zionist leadership, since the end of the Second World War until 1952, was responsible for the failure of negotiations that could have led to peace accords. Flapan's book posed a problem to the extent that the author felt politically engaged, as he clearly indicated in the introduction. Even though his conclusions were amply supported by facts and references, some passages from his essay made it appear like a political and moral pamphlet.

The three other essays that undermined the legitimacy of the official discourse were works of a more academic tone. Avi Shlaim, Ilan Pappé and Benny Morris each received their doctorate from a renowned British university. The Israeli research that relied on the Anglo-Saxon scientific world in the humanities and social sciences could not deny them. In different ways, their essays confirmed Simha Flapan's arguments, and sometimes went even farther. Shlaim, using British and Israeli documents declassified in the early 1980s, focused on the contacts between the Zionist movement and King Abdullah of Jordan. Against the foundation myth adopted by Israeli national memory, which postulated a coalition of Arab countries to destroy the State of Israel, he drew a complex portrait of concurrent strategic interests between the Zionist leadership and the Hashemite monarch that finally led to the partition of the Palestinian State that never saw the light of day. Ilan Pappé completed this argument by highlighting the active role of the British Empire in this process and by analyzing the relationship of military forces. He refuted the Israeli consensus opinion that had always presented the 1948 conflict as the small Jewish David against the giant Arab Goliath. In the end, the result of the war faithfully reflected the real relationship of forces on the ground, Pappé confirmed, and he elicited the condemnation of the "authorized" Israeli historians.[10]

Yet it was Benny Morris who drew the most ire and interest in dealing with the Palestinian problem. For many years, in Israel, it was taught that the majority of refugees had voluntarily abandoned their houses during the 1948 War to escape to areas controlled by

Arab armies, motivated by the slogans and propaganda of their leaders on Arab radio stations. Morris dismantled the story and refuted the myth on the basis of a long list of facts gleaned from recently declassified archives and files. There was no Arab call for exodus. On the contrary, the instructions were to remain in place. The 700,000 Palestinians who followed the path of exile did so because they were afraid of being killed; massacres had taken place, and not only in Deir Yassin. Among the fugitives, many were simply chased away. Even if Israeli leaders never gave formal orders to expulse the majority of the Arab population hat fell under its control, on the ground, commanders did their best to empty entire villages of their inhabitants with the "benediction" of political authorities. The idea of this transfer was not foreign to the Zionist movement, even if it was difficult for many of its leaders to say it openly: they always preferred having the British do the work in their place.[11]

The creation of the State of Israel became a foundational historic fact and the cause of the injustice against the non-Jewish population. Put in the context of the 1987 Palestinian uprising, this assessment began to gain more widespread acknowledgement among intellectual circles. While Avi Shlaim's and Ilan Pappé's books were not given a Hebrew translation, Benny Morris' work, appearing in 1991 with a major publisher, attracted immediate interest. The authorized historians reacted strongly and attempted to minimize both the novelty and the credibility of his critical arguments. Dozens of essays, articles and even a book were written to refute the facts or at least attenuate the impact of the conclusions resulting from them.[12] Yet before institutional historiography could recover from this revisionist attack on the interpretation of the 1948 War, it was under a new assault.

Facing the Survivors

Tom Segev, a journalist with a doctorate in history and the author of two books on history, published *The Seventh Million*[13] in 1993. In it, the victims of the Zionist enterprise were not the refugees of the Nakba but the survivors of the Shoah. The "relative" but inevitable wrong suffered by the Palestinians had always been justified by the fact that Zionist institutions saved the survivors of the Shoah.

In 1977, the publication of Shabatai Beit Avi's controversial book had already critiqued the relative inaction and indifference of Zionist leaders towards the annihilation of European Judaism.[14] During the 1970s, criticism of this kind from outside the margins of the historiographical field—Beit Zvi was an engineer by profession, without connection to university circles or the press—was only met with silence. At the beginning of the 1990s, however, public opinion had matured and could accept analyses of the complex relationships between Zionism and the Shoah. Tom Segev, the linguist Yosef Grodzinsky who had followed in his path and others placed the accent not only on the inability of Zionist institutions to assist the Jews of Europe during the war—a fact that had already been analyzed by more traditional researchers—but also their reticence to provide the necessary aid when their place of refuge was somewhere other than "Eretz Israel."[15] The possibilities of rescue were limited but these refugees were not a priority for Ben-Gurion and the Zionist authorities because it was much more important to concentrate every effort and all financial resources on pursuing colonization and building the State. The relationship between these authorities and the survivors of the Second World War who immigrated to Palestine under the Palestinian Mandate, which later became the State of Israel, was not without exploitation and paternalism. In the Zionist community of Palestine before the arrival of the great waves of immigration, the young Hebrew sentiment did not hide its disdain for the weakness, the lack of "virility" and national pride among the Jews who had survived the Shoah or for their cultural heritage. And while the survivors of the Holocaust faced disdain, immigrants from Islamic countries were the victims of an aggressive and systematic policy that attempted to erase their original identities. Forced to hide or repress the specificities of their Arab culture, they fell back on their religious practices, the last vestige perhaps of their Jewish identity.

Unlike the factors that favored the revision of the theses on the circumstances and consequences of the 1948 War, most information that raised questions about the attitude of Zionist institutions towards the Shoah and the waves of immigrants that arrived after the proclamation of independence came from official publications open to the public, from press archives, personal diaries and memoirs. The change in historical sensibilities in the 1990s was not directly (or not solely) dependent on the opening of archives or the discovery of new documents, but to an intellectual malaise related to the weight of official memory and its control over Israeli historiography.

Moreover, the historiographical discussion, like the debates held in the public arena, primarily concerned political issues. The 1948 War, the Shoah and immigration to Israel were generally examined from "on high" by the political elite, and while the actions of the latter were subject to a rigorous critique, the changes taking place in large sectors of society were obscured. And no serious work of historical anthropology or cultural history on the questions raised by the new critiques ever appeared. While it had an impact on the development of public memory in Israel in the 1990s, this historiographical turn did not offer any new methodological or conceptual contribution. Some critics tried to put forward their "post-modern" approaches to distinguish themselves from historiographic positivism, but a study of their texts reveals the use of conventional materials, mainly from diplomatic sources, and the production of "realist" discourses based on purely empirical methods.

The print and audiovisual media took an interest in this contestation of political institutions. The 1948 War, the Shoah and immigration became hot topics in the consciousness of the Israeli public and it is not surprising that this past caused some heated exchanges. However, in the end this turn was more concerned with questioning the nature of Zionist colonization since the end of the 19th century and on the perception of the Jewish past as a national history. No professional historian entered the polemic on these two fundamental questions.

Zionism and Colonization

The radically new interpretations of social and economic history of the Zionist enterprise grew out of the new generation of sociologists. In 1983, Baruch Kimmerling had already published his pioneering doctoral thesis, *Zionism and Territory*, which he had defended at the Hebrew University of Jerusalem, where he obtained a teaching position. But it was published in the United States and never appeared in Israel. The work is socio-historical in nature, following the best Weberian tradition, and offers an original explanation of the social and political relationships of force in Palestine during the British mandate. To understand a society of new immigrants, Kimmerling posits, the institutional explanations related to the implanted community that are commonly adopted in sociology and history in Israel are insufficient. A serious socio-historical approach must take on the analysis of the spatial conditions in which Zionist colonization took place and compare them to other types of modern colonization.

Unlike North America or Australia, for example, immigration to Palestine settled in an inhabited area with a relatively high population density and these conditions shaped its specific modalities. The collective socialism that was the pride of the Zionist enterprise came from the intellectual idealism of its leading figures and especially from the specific needs of an immigrant society locked in a bitter struggle for land acquisition. The process of territorial acquisition was not built on the family unit or individually, as in other models of colonization, but through groups organized in collectivities and centralized institutions. This was the basis for the socialist trend in the Zionist enterprise and then in the State of Israel; it also explained the State's control of the economy and the production of cultural goods. The development of Israeli society, culture and political mentality cannot be understood without taking into account this particular aspect of its colonization and, *a fortiori*, the prolonged, antagonistic confrontation with the local Arab population.

This historical starting point is at the center of Baruch Kimmerling's thought. When the great debate began at the end of the 1980s, he became one of the protagonists. *The Israeli State and Society: Boundaries and Frontiers*, a collection of essays he edited in the United States in 1989, became one of the books that marked a decisive turning point.[16] Despite reserves about a few passages, his book on the history of the Palestinian people, written in 1993 with Joel Migdal, represents one of the most courageous and insightful works by an Israeli scholar on his neighboring people.[17] His essays on militarism and on the development of collective identities and national consciousness published during the 1990s gave the "post-Zionist" revision a sociocultural depth that had been missing from most of the other participants in the debate. His theoretical and conceptual contributions to Israeli historiography introduced elements of intelligibility that had been missing in the discursive practices of the Israeli public.[18]

With the ideological and institutional weaknesses of historians specializing in Zionism and Israel, sociology produced scholars who were able to provide a critical and comparative approach. *Zionism and Territory* was not the only dissenting work against the official discourse that avoided traditional concepts. *Land, Labor and the Origins of the Israeli-Palestinian Conflict*, mentioned above, helped complete Baruch Kimmerling's work in several ways. Instead of only dealing with the conquest of land, Gershon Shafir preferred dealing with the internal development of labor relationships in the Zionist enterprise. During the Ottoman period of Zionist colonization, the labor market was already characterized by the distinction between Jewish and Arab workers. After the failure to reproduce the type of colonization used in Algeria, which consisted of exploiting an Arab labor force that Jewish laborers could not compete with, the Zionist union—the Histadrut—turned to the settlement model practiced by Germany in regions of Eastern Prussia at the end of the 19th century: German workers were encouraged to settle where Polish farmers were a threat to colonization. Zionism deliberately copied this model and it inspired the idea of a colonizing corporation later known as a kibbutz. The kibbutz land belonged to the new nation and was solely entrusted to Jewish workers. In this way, free competition between farmers was frozen and the concept of "Hebrew labor" became a reality.

Zionism, which had become socialist out of the necessities of colonization, succeeded in pushing Arab workers outside the
agricultural sector of the Jewish community. The movement,
despite its dreams of territorial expansion measured by divine
promise, preferred a demographic majority defined by the Jewish
"ethnos" to a geographic space without a clear national character.

The struggle to acquire land and the efforts to "conquer labor"
were reflected in the political choices and cultural practices of the
Zionist community in Palestine. The social history of this space
cannot ignore the colonizing and national origins of the conflict.
Against the "authorized" historians of the history of the Jewish people, Baruch Kimmerling and Gershon Shafir were able to use a
comparative method to lay the foundations of a history of Zionism
at the beginning of "secularization." The most intriguing aspect is
precisely in the use of patented modes of sociological expression—
using models and parameters—to legitimize, in the eyes of the
university, the abandon of the particularism where traditional historiography had wanted to confine the history of the Zionist
movement. Undermining this historiography's determination to
maintain its unique status took advantage of both the principle of
particularity as an axis of research into historical phenomena and
of the non-existence of a "department of Jewish sociology," which
allowed the creation of a critical and analogical historiography.

The new colonization after the 1967 War also had a strong influence on the work of the two sociologists. The history of the 1970s,
with the hasty establishment of Israeli settlements in the heart of the
Palestinian territories, shed light on the beginnings of the Zionist
enterprise and provided a means for understanding them. The similarities and differences between the settlements before 1948 and
those after 1967 put a comparative historical vision into perspective,

one that had not been available to Israeli scholars until the 1980s. One might say that subjects dealing with local history over a "long duration" were harder to accept than questions of memory or politics. Understanding the Zionist enterprise as a process of colonization made possible by its image in the context of European colonial expansion between the end of the 19th century and the early 20th century was too radical a paradigmatic leap for some.

Jewish Past between Religious History and National Construction

In *Jewish State or Israeli Nation* by Boaz Evron, published in 1988, was the only essay on this question written and published in Hebrew in the 1980s. There were only rare critiques and the silence surrounding its publication reveals the way the Israeli university world works. An independent intellectual more than a historian, Boaz Evron had shown a daring and non-conformist mind in his intention to include ancient Yahwist history, Jewish history and modern Israeli history in a single movement. From Heinrich Graetz in the 19th century to Simon Dubnov in the early 20th to Ben Zion Dinur for the Israeli period, the history of the Jewish past had already been the object of several works of synthesis. Yet until Evron's book appeared, no one had tried to write an alternative history with the central objective of highlighting the deconstruction of the characteristic linearity of the "history of Israel."

To the main question: "Is it possible to see the Jews as a territorial people cast out at the time of the destruction of the second Temple and survived as a national entity for two thousand years?" he responded in the negative. No people is eternal. Throughout history, peoples have formed and disappeared, and the Jews are no exception. While in Antiquity at the time of the kingdoms of Israel and Judah, a people shared a common culture, the Jewish religion was formed when that people was divided and the cultural elite exiled in Babylon made Judaism a collective identity, tying the limits on its members to the beliefs of the faithful. A fringe of this new tradition developed separately into "ethnic" and separatist tendencies—the books of Ezra and Nehemia are its ideological reflections—but this avant-garde monotheistic belief also became the first universal religion to practice proselytism. The growth of the Jewish population in the Roman Empire cannot be explained without recognizing this dynamic in ancient Judaism. Thanks to these proselytizing tendencies, deep set in all monotheistic beliefs, Jewish communities emerged in North Africa, Yemen, and later in the Caucasus. The retreat of Judaism and its defeat by its two "daughters"—Christianity and Islam—were primarily the result of the fear of the rabbis to participate in mass conversions that would threaten their status as the cultural elite.

Taking a working hypothesis inspired by Max Weber and supported by his "Canaanite" ideological training, Boaz Evron establishes that starting with the dispersion of the Jewish people, Judaism can be seen historically as a diversified religious culture transmitted by religious castes that were always dependent on the societies where they lived. The *Galut* or "exile" was never a geographical state, as Zionist historiography presented it, but an existential state in which the definition of the Jewish essence was developed over time. Any attempt to reconstruct the history of the Jews as the national history of a people exiled from their land and descended from a single origin is subject to irresolvable internal contradictions. The Jews never showed common secular cultural norms and always integrated the language and economy of other populations. With little concern for settling in separate places of habitation, their profound aspiration for the Holy Land never led to a massive emigration movement (except for the minor messianic currents rejected by Judaism).

Only in Eastern Europe, in the context of a sizeable demographic concentration and a determinant linguistic and cultural alienation, was the Yiddish people formed, in parallel with a weakening of religious belief. A secular culture was developed within the Yiddish people that was radically different from the surrounding populations. Zionism was born out of this people through its rejection of the nascent nationalism of its neighbors. This minority current, the direct descendant of the Yiddish people's distress and not from an ahistorical national identity, began the national colonizing undertaking that led to the birth of the Israeli nation.

Boaz Evron uses many concepts that are subject to debate. He does not always respect the rules of empirical research and his use of secondary sources sometimes leads him to draw hasty conclusions. But his theoretical approach and audacity produced impressive and innovative results that have not received all of the attention they deserve. The fact that his book appeared outside the academy meant that it was ostracized by the institutional structure of Jewish history studies, which stifled any attempt to follow-up on this research within the Israeli university framework.

Showing exceptional perseverance in critiquing the foundations of institutional historiography, a young sociologist from the Ben-Gurion University of Beer Sheva, Uri Ram, studied history before publishing an essay on Ben Zion Dinur, the Israeli Lavisse,[19] in 1995. This Zionist historian was one of the two founders of the Jewish History department at the Hebrew University of Jerusalem. As Minister of National Education of the young State of Israel from 1951 to 1955, he defined the history programs in the public school system. Uri Ram attempted to dismantle the paradigm of Zionist history by reconstructing Dinur's historiological path until its completion. Dinur's goal was to give empirical content to the founding principle of Zionism stated in the 1947 declaration of establishment of the State:

> Eretz-Israel was the birthplace of the Jewish people. [...] After being forcibly exiled from their land, the people kept faith with it throughout their Dispersion and never ceased to pray and hope for their return to it and for the restoration in it of their political freedom. Impelled by this historic and traditional attachment, Jews strove in every successive generation to re-establish themselves in their ancient homeland. In recent decades they returned in their masses.

This teleological and organic principle, based on a perception of the past, was already present in the essays that Ben Zion Dinur wrote in the 1930s. Twenty years later, official history validated it. For Dinur, the changes in and the diversity of Jewish experience over several centuries of life in "exile," in other words, the concrete histories, were only appearances. The national consciousness and particularly the relationship to the homeland was the unchanging kernel that remained latent until blossoming in the modern era. To seal the ties between the wandering nation and the abandoned homeland, Dinur modified the traditional periods of "exile." For him, it started in the 7th century (of the Christian era) with the Muslim conquest and ended with the advent of Rabbi Judah he-Hasid in 1700. On one hand, he extended the Jewish presence in the country and reduced the Arab period on the other.

Uri Ram did not only attempt to contradict Dinur's positions; he also replaced his historical thinking in the context of the formation of the collective memory. He postulated that until recently all Israeli historians espoused nationalism. The historical discourse was organized in view of the construction of a national memory and everything that did not serve this project was forgotten and abandoned. We should not deduce from this that Uri Ram believes a neutral, scientific history free from all value judgments is possible. He does not call for a positivist history that ignores ideological pressures to replace institutional historiography. The Beer Sheva sociologist hopes for a post-Zionist historiography, not one developed on the basis of an ahistorical Jewish essence but based on a critical approach to a concrete Israeli identity. This alternative historical program would mean, according to Ram, that Israel had passed from the stage of a national society to that of a civil society. And the changes to the historiographical perspective would be one aspect of the transformation of the overall national culture that seems to be underway.

Too Close to See Clearly?

The political processes and the cultural evolution of the 1990s confirmed Uri Ram's "republican" and enlightened project on many points. The Oslo Accords gave rise to a climate of calm and serenity for a year or two. Many thought that the Israeli-Palestinian conflict had reached its end. Dissident intellectuals and some of their readers found themselves taken by the naïve belief that Israel was entering the post-Zionist era. Different positions and opinions on Israeli history were more widely published, encouraging critical expression. New historiographical discoveries entered the news, corroborated by archeological findings: they found that the biblical accounts of the conquest of the Land of Canaan and the Kingdom of David were less than accurate.[20] Israeli society seemed ready to accept the reevaluation of its founding myths.

Historical research did not benefit very much from this favorable climate. Only one study came out of the ideological debates of the mid-1990s.[21] Those behind the post-Zionist debate invested more in polemics in the media than in consolidating their position in the domains of historical production. And on the whole this production remained largely unchanged. The Jewish History departments continued to produce, with generous university grants. The "Post-Zionists" had many followers with the exception of Jewish history and Israeli history, where the turn has yet to occur—they continue to reproduce the old paradigm's conceptual mechanisms.

A study of the composition of the teaching and research personnel during those years reveals that the recruitment of people of Palestinian origin hardly increased. While the Arab population represents 20% of the population of Israel, the percentage of Arab professors in the university systems is only 2%. At the University of Tel Aviv, the history departments—Jewish, General and Middle Eastern History—employ no Arab researchers. Because of this fact there is no joint historical research on the country's past by Israeli Jews and Israeli Arabs.

This institutional immobility is not surprising. Despite the liberalization of political culture started during the 1970s and 1980s, the nature of Israeli nationality underwent no fundamental change. As I mentioned in the introduction, the national identity pictured by the Zionist movement at the end of the 19th century was based on the principle of the nation-spirit and not the national-contract, with similarities to the German concept of *Volk*.[22] The process of colonization in Palestine under the mandate maintained the ethnic definition, instead of the collective identity, and it finally became the cornerstone national definition of the State of Israel. This political entity saw itself and still sees itself as the State of all Jews in the world.

Although the 1960s began with the first limited Israelization of public culture and sensibilities, the 1967 War and the passage of massive numbers of Palestinians under Israeli military control caused the government to revisit the question of ethnicity. With territorial expansion bringing with it a major demographic "threat," the demarcation lines of ethnic-religious identity were consolidated and reinforced instead of dissipating. As paradoxical as it may seem, the spread of political and cultural pluralism was paralleled by an increasing ethnicization of State identity.

And while there was a noticeable change in mentality after the Oslo Accords, it led to few political acts. The period following the Accords, when the post-Zionist polemic reached its height, was also a period of increased colonization in the occupied territories. From Yitzhak Rabin's assassination in 1994 until the end of the last century, the number of colonists almost doubled, with support from every Israeli government. The newly arrived colonists in the territories during the "Oslo years" equaled the number of Israelis who had settled there over the previous 25 years. And with the arrival of more than a million immigrants from countries in Eastern Europe—a fifth of the total population—we can assume that many of the new colonists were also new immigrants.

With the outbreak of the Al-Aqsa Intifada and the national coalition of Ariel Sharon taking power, the media positions of the

"Post-Zionists" disappeared. The liberal tolerance that had started to appear began to retreat. It may be temporary but in the meantime there is nothing to indicate that nationalist thought will not prosper. In times of armed conflict, the intellectual "muses," including the historiographers, don the traits of intense nationalism. It all increases the difficulty of evaluating the strength of the new elements of memory proposed over the past decade. The violence of the renewed conflict prevents us from seeing the limits of the current structure of memory and it would be imprudent to draw any definitive conclusions.

"When we are too far or too close we cannot see properly," wrote Pascal. The historicization of the historiographical and intellectual debate in the early 21st century may not elicit the passions that it did at first, but it still draws too much passion for us to be able to do a full appraisal of its implications and its impact on ideological traditions. What traces will it leave in Israeli memory? Many of the "authorized" historians see it as a passing fancy. And perhaps we should take full measure of the assertion that historical myths only last until they are replaced by others.

Bernard Lazare, the First French Zionist

Equilibrium alone destroys and annuls force. If we know in what way society is unbalanced, we must do what we can to add weight to the lighter scale. Although the weight may consist of evil, in handling it in this intention, perhaps we do not become defiled. But we must have formed a conception of this equilibrium and be ever ready to change sides like justice, "that fugitive from the camp of conquerors."
— Simone Weil, *Gravity and Grace.*

For Péguy, he was a "saint"; for Léon Blum, a prophet; and for others... yet until recently, Bernard Lazare's writing had mainly been published by questionable publishers with an unsettling interest in Judaism.[1] Although a circle of the Zionist Left in Paris took his name, in Israel, where street signs memorialize the names of all of the founders and leaders of the Zionist movement, even the most marginal ones, and non-Jews like Zola and Jaurès have "their" street for their role in the Dreyfus Affair, Bernard Lazare's name is nowhere to be found. The work of the Dreyfus' pioneering defender has almost been completely forgotten.[2] The name of one of the very first French Zionists has disappeared from the collective memory of the nation that he longed to see "resurrected."

Saints, heroes and prophets generally enjoy eternal glory in the collective memory, which is how they become sanctified. Bernard Lazare is not an easy fit for these categories, although a few hagiographic attempts have been made.[3] It should be noted that Lazare did everything for posterity to lose track of him except die young and almost penniless.

The paths that Bernard Lazare followed seemed like disappointments to his various, temporary partners: a disappointment for symbolism when he abandoned poetry for journalism, a deep disappointment for the anti-Semites who had considered him to be one of their "companions" after his early literary works, an apparent disappointment for the anarchists when he began to participate in Zionist political activities and an even greater disappointment for the Zionists who had begun to see him as the symbol of renewed Jewish pride. At the end of his brief life, he was even able to disappoint the victorious Dreyfusards who kept him away from the victory celebrations. Lazare was like a porcupine pricking anyone who came too close. He did not seem to leave any time for time to change him but was always changing ahead of the times.

Contemporary interest in Bernard Lazare is not primarily in these aspects of his life: he was not a leading Symbolist author, even though some of his criticism is not without interest;[4] he was not an innovative libertarian thinker, despite the cutting wit and brio of some of his articles;[5] like Theodor Herzl, the founder of political Zionism, he was not a particularly penetrating Zionist ideologue. Lazare still captures our interest for a completely different reason: he was one of the only intellectuals in Western Europe at the end of the

19th century who developed an independent ideological conception of the modern Jewish national consciousness.

While the Jewish origin and culture of many intellectuals in Central and Eastern Europe led them to Zionism, such cases were rare in England, France, Holland and Belgium. The development of Western liberal democracy, despite the rise of anti-Semitism and racism that punctuated it was characterized by a political conception of the nation in terms of assimilation and fusion rather than separation and purification, which opened cultural and mental horizons dominated by their universal aspect. This political culture contributed to erasing the distinctive traits of a specific Jewish culture, unlike the situation in Eastern Europe. The context in Western Europe did not encourage the formation of Zionist thought, which makes it all the more interesting to study the original sensibility of authors like Bernard Lazare, André Spire and Israel Zangwill.

Bernard Lazare's works offer at least two other aspects of particular interest: a constant tension to neutralize politics by perpetually developing an ethical impulse and his intent to understand the nation using libertarian categories. Even though there was a great distance between his thoughts and practice for both of these issues, the sensiblity and questions expressed by Lazare deserve further study.

Lazare Marcus Manassé Bernard, who later took the pen name Bernard Lazare, was born into a wealthy Jewish family in Nîmes in 1865. After high school and a brief period of activity in the Société littéraire et artistique de Nîmes, young Bernard left for Paris at age 21 to enroll in the science of religions at the École Pratique de Hautes Études. However, the young man from Nîmes was quickly drawn to the symbolist poets of the 1880s. He tried his hand at various publications, contributing to *Entretiens politiques et littéraires.*[6] In it, he attacked the Parnassians and Naturalism and also published racist articles against Jews in Eastern Europe.

His symbolist activities brought him closer to anarchist circles and in a few years he became one of the most well known Parisian libertarian publicists. However, his new radical politics did not bring an end to his exploration of the Jewish question; in 1894, he published an important work called *L'Antisémitisme, son histoire et ses causes* [Antisemitism, its History and its Causes],[7] where remnants of his past judeophobic views are mixed pell-mell with expressions of new philo-Semitism.

As early as 1895, Bernard Lazare was convinced of Dreyfus' innocence; he became the first Dreyfusard outside the Captain's family. In 1896, he had a brochure published in Brussels called *"Un erreur judiciaire. La vérité sur l'Affaire Dreyfus"* [A Miscarriage of Justice. The Truth about the Dreyfus Affair].[8] From that date until the amnesty decision in 1899, he spent the better part of his time and his pen in the fight to reverse the decision. While remaining intensely active in journalism as well as literary pursuits and circles, he resolutely engaged in action against any signs of anti-Semitism. He joined Herzl in calling for the rebirth of Jewish national rights and in 1898 became a member of the executive committee of the Zionist Congress.[9]

As the republican-Dreyfusard camp won its first victories and the Zionist movement solidified its organization and its political line, this "anarchist-Zionist" began to feel marginalized. The late arrivals to the Dreyfus camp tried to keep the demanding, non-conformist Lazare under wraps; the direction taken by the new political elite was increasingly foreign to him. In 1902, Lazare, an anticlerical hardliner, eviscerated the government's prosecution of congregations in the *Cahiers de la quinzaine*.[10]

His relationship with the Zionist Congress also began to deteriorate in 1899. Bernard Lazare refused to accept the policy of courting the Ottoman sultan and severely criticized the fact that one of the first steps of the new Jewish movement was to start a bank.[11] Without abandoning his Jewish national pride, Lazare left the Zionist Congress. Over the next few years, the last years of his short life, he made efforts to help Jews who were being persecuted in Eastern Europe. Alone and in pain, he died from cancer in 1903.

The first question raised by this brief biographical summary could be the source of the Judeophobia found in his first intellectual productions. There is no lack of interpretations. Some see it as the characteristic "self-loathing" of Jews who work to eliminate their original identity in order to gain the approval of the cultural world that they long to enter. There is a long list of figures of Jewish origin whose writings are dotted with pejorative statements about the Jewish religion, its followers and even their non-religious descendants: from Karl Marx to Walter Rathenau, from Ferdinand Lassalle to Simone Weil to name only a few.[12]

The error in this psychological interpretation is its static conception of Jewish identity, as if there were a clear and precise Jewish essence within every subject of Jewish origin. Marx, whose father had converted to Christianity, should have felt Jewish despite his lack of interest, making him an anti-Semite. The same type of interpretation is applied to Bernard Lazare as a young Jew arriving in Paris, where his passport into French intellectual society required the renunciation of his origins, leading to his painful "self-loathing."[13]

While Marx's case is up for debate—his prejudice against Judaism seems remarkably similar to the other non-Jewish "young Hegelians"—Bernard Lazare fits the "self-loathing" theory even less. Lazare never went so far as to renounce his origins and his collection of political and literary writings reveal a personality free of "self-loathing." As a "French Israelite," he did not shy away from expressing his derision and sometimes hatred of others and he hardly tried to conceal his own identity. Placing the accent on his status as a Sephardic French Israelite, he showed no hesitation in saying he was Jewish or to sing the praises of a persecuted people.

In fact, even in his earliest writings, Bernard Lazare attempts to clarify his identity, which is not the same as self-denial or loathing. He represents a case of those who are not necessarily born Jewish but who come to be Jewish, in particular with help from anti-Semites.

There was a certain Judeophobia in symbolist and anarchist circles inherited from populist traditions and also the newly developing racial "science," which was behind the "return" to anti-Jewish expressions at the time. Bernard Lazare was not an isolated case in the poisonous atmosphere of the Panama scandal and the Dreyfus Affair. Like his non-Jewish contemporaries, he was also carrying a form of anti-Semitism. The waves of immigration from Russia following the pogroms of the 1880s, the economic instability of the period and the rise of mass democracy were all factors that fed political anti-Semitism in Central and Western Europe.[14]

The intellectual elite reacted like the political classes. The definition and rejection of the Other were no longer defined using "reactionary" religious categories but with "progressive" conceptual terms in keeping with the spirit of the times. A "perversion" of positivism into biological determinism penetrated several thinkers, be they conservative or democrats, neo-liberals or socialists and anarchists. In an intellectual trend sweeping Europe, history began to rely on biology.

A young symbolist at the time, Bernard Lazare like many French Israelites expressed the distance between himself and this rude, foreign Other who emphasized the "Frenchness" of Israelites. The Other, the foreigner was embodied by the Jews from Eastern Europe who were trying to emigrate to the West. There was nothing in common between these Jews and Israelites, according to Lazare:

> External circumstances, environmental influences, historical causes and climate are not sufficient to explain such differences between people of a common origin. Only deviations due to mixtures, changes in constitution, modifications of cerebral matter can justify them.... Russian Jews, French Jews, German Jews and English Jews, Polish Jews and Italian Jews are separated by the same distance that separate Slavs from Germans, Latins from Saxons.[15]

According to Lazare, one should avoid confusing the two races: on the one side, there is the pure and simple race of Portuguese Jews, and on the other the race of Ashkenazi Jews bastardized by their ties to the Huns, their characteristic cranial shape and their repugnant mentality:

> "Believing that this division is based on random geographical circumstances would be a mistake; it is based on profound differences in ethnic constitution, character and morality. The Portuguese who joined with people of the Latin race (those who are in Holland or England are immigrants) belong to the type anthropologists call dolichocephalic. Germans, who are more appropriately called Tartars, belong to the brachycephalic type; in the first centuries of this era, they encountered the massive lirachycephalic immigration and the Caucasus was the

center of their fusion." As for the Portuguese, "the Semitic type is predominant in them; they are most often rather tall, with a strongly shaped nose, fine curly hair and clear eyes. Germans are generally small, pallid with dirty red hair or dirty yellow hair in Bohemia, sparse beards and lifeless eyes. When you meet them in the lower classes of Poland, Russia, Galicia or in the ghettos of Germany, you find yourself in the presence of an unclean creature dressed in rags, viscous and repugnant in appearance, speaking a strange Judeo-German patois."[16]

France should close its doors to this new invasion of Huns, and Israelites should avoid any solidarity with them.

Bernard Lazare's misfortune, and the misfortune of the majority of French Israelites, was that anti-Semites did not make this distinction and saw all Jews as coming from a single, fixed origin. There were two consequences to this position: most French Israelites felt obliged to insist even more on their Frenchness while on the contrary, Lazare, as a proud non-conformist, felt compelled to think further about his identity, expand it and even change it. Thus the French Israelites who saw their origin as a point of departure became French Jews whose background represented an existential finality. (A similar process affected French Israelites after the June 1967 War, albeit in a completely different context.)

The mental and intellectual transformation of Bernard Lazare the young anarchist did not take place overnight. From 1892 to 1894, he focused on the history of anti-Judaism. The result was the first systematic investigation of anti-Semitism, a work that was also incorporated into the anti-Semitic sphere. At this point in his writings, Lazare had already left behind his first anti-Judaism based on biological determinism, which allowed the publisher Pierre

Guillaume to publish his work in the 1980s with unveiled excitement, while unfortunately stating that "At no time will you find in him (Bernard Lazare) the slightest racial or racist interpretation or the slightest essentialist interpretation."[17]

Unlike Germany, racial and biological anti-Semitism were not wide-spread in France. The nationalist aggression that served as a foundation for this type of anti-Semitism in other countries did not take hold in France at the turn of the century because of the Alsace-Lorraine question: every nationalist of note had to call for the return of the lost provinces, and express his or her hatred of the German occupiers, who were Aryans to boot! The situation made it hard for Aryan theories to find an echo. The tenets of French racism also made it difficult to assimilate Alsatians purely and simply into a French ethnicity. This may be one of the explanations for the fact that French racism had few biological connotations, alongside the hegemonic heritage of Jacobinism and the weight of Catholicism.

Bernard Lazare did not pursue "Israelite" racism for very long either. While coming close to some of Marx's historical concepts (without adhering to political Marxism),[18] he eliminated the previous racist and Darwinist categories from his articles. Some anti-Semitic ingredients remained, however, which allowed Drumont and later Xavier Vallat to have a positive reaction to Lazare's book on anti-Semitism.[19] The basic theory behind his essay is found in the first chapter: because anti-Judaism has appeared at different times in a variety of societies,

> it must needs be that the general causes of anti-Semitism have always resided in Israel itself, and not in those who antagonized it. This does not mean that justice was always on the side

of Israel's persecutors, or that they did not indulge in all the extremes born of hatred; it is merely asserted that the Jews were themselves, in part, at least, the cause of their own ills.[20]

This type of statement is the equivalent of saying that the skin color of Africans is the cause of racism against Blacks. For Lazare, there is always the question of historical responsibility; anti-Semitism always appears after a period of Jewish exclusivism:

> Why was he ill-treated and hated alike and in turn by the Alexandrians and the Romans, by the Persians and the Arabs, by the Turks and the Christian nations? Because, everywhere up to our own days the Jew was an unsociable being. Why was he unsociable? Because he was exclusive, and his exclusiveness was both political and religious, or rather he held fast to his political and religious cult, to his law.[21]

His declaration is not invalidated by the fact that this kind of situation never occurred in the past but by its abusive generalization concerning the past, its imprecision concerning the modern era and its generally ahistorical character. The foundations of political anti-Semitism and racism in the 19th century are found more in the process of modernization than in the "asocial" character of the Jews who on the contrary were on a path of integration to and assimilation with the social environment. Jewish exclusivism, religious in origin, was being diluted while leaving more or less pronounced traces of cultural differences. But these differences were judged to be untenable in the context of national cultural conformism, and were influenced as well by the feeling of insecurity that is one of the characteristics of modern collective identities.

Bernard Lazare was aware of some aspects of this situation, as the last part of his book reveals despite its peremptory statements and hasty conclusions. It was the work of a harried essayist and not the work of a historian. Attributing an asocial character to the Jewish people no matter what the time period has no more value than conferring a particular "revolutionary spirit" on them, which Lazare sometimes does just as lightly.[22]

Characteristically for a person on the Left during his time, Bernard Lazare concluded his unprecedented research by predicting a transformation of anti-Semitism after the complete assimilation of the Jews:

> Such is the irony of things that anti-Semitism which everywhere is the creed of the conservative class, of those who accuse the Jews of having worked hand in hand with the Jacobins of 1789 and the Liberals and Revolutionists of the nineteenth century, this very anti-Semitism is acting, in fact, as an ally of the Revolution. Drumont in France, Pattai in Hungary, Stoecker and von Boeckel in Germany are co-operating with the very demagogues and revolutionists whom they believe they are attacking. This anti-Semitic movement, in its origin reactionary, has become transformed and is acting now for the advantage of the revolutionary cause. Anti-Semitism stirs up the middle class, the small tradesmen, and sometimes the peasant, against the Jewish capitalist, but in doing so it gently leads them toward Socialism, prepares them for anarchy, infuses in them a hatred for all capitalists, and, more than that, for capital in the abstract.[23]

Yet even as his book was published, Lazare the anarchist began to have his first doubts about this optimistic prognosis. The resolution of the "first" Dreyfus Affair was the backdrop for his misgivings.[24] But it took something more to cause this libertarian to nuance or feel shaken in his belief in progress and to send him to war against all forms of anti-Semitism.

The "first" Dreyfus Affair corresponded to the Captain's trial in 1894. The "second" Dreyfus Affair covered the campaign following the publication of "J'accuse" by Émile Zola in early 1898. The "first" Affair entered the Jewish collective national memory as a founding event, while France tends to celebrate the struggle that started in 1898 and that led to the victory of universal human rights. Bernard Lazare disappeared into a forgotten "no man's land" between these two collective national memories; historically, however, he served as a kind of liaison between the two periods, after being the first link in the chain of intellectuals whose actions made the start of the "second" Affair possible.

The paradox is that while the appearance of an organized Zionist movement preceded the formation of the Dreyfusard camp, Bernard Lazare was a Dreyfusard before being a Zionist and remained a Dreyfusard even as he became a Zionist. Nelly Wilson has retraced Lazare's itinerary to becoming the first Dreyfusard in a sympathetic biography.[25] The libertarian with an increasing attachment to Judaism associated strongly with the officer persecuted for being Jewish at a time when even someone of the stature of Jean Jaurès believed that the Captain deserved to hang. A few years later, Lazare expressed his disillusion with the time:

> I had seen Jaurès before the attacks in *La Petite République*....
> I found Jaurès to be very cold, almost hostile. Either he had not read or he could not logically see that I was right or he was hesitating for political reasons. I had the occasion to see him

again that year and even wrote to him. I could not get him to understand the social importance of the question or its interest for the Socialist cause. To say nothing of the insults and injuries or the accusations. From that day, I was spared nothing of the attitude of the press. From one day to the next, I became a pariah.[26]

The solitary trek through the desert of Parisian "progressivist" circles after the first trial was also the last stage of the journey that brought Bernard Lazare to his historic meeting with Theodor Herzl and Jewish national sentiment. The French Left, anti-Dreyfusard or indifferent to the Affair from 1894 to 1897, disappointed the Jewish intellectual just as France, the country of human rights, disturbed many Central and Eastern European Jews with its wave of anti-Semitism during the same years. One option had been eliminated and the image of a bright future grew dim.[27]

In his conversion to national Judaism, Bernard Lazare did not abandon the radical utopianism that distinguished him from other intellectuals who were also searching for their Jewish identity. His unyielding utopianism may be what made him a Zionist: his demonstrative anarchism may have led him to the idea that an apologetic defense against anti-Semitism might not be enough and that it was necessary to proclaim Jewish specificity with pride. Accepting Zionism in Paris in 1897 was not as easy as it was in 1967 or 1987:[28] it meant adopting a completely marginal position among intellectuals and going against the dominant ideas of the period.

The crisis of anarchy and its ebb in the late 1890s could have pushed Bernard Lazare to join one of the movements of political socialism, become a journalist supporting the newly developing unions or retreat into withered anarchism. But he took a totally different direction. The libertarian flame burning within him continued to push him to revolt, but the anti-Semite problem made him turn from the route followed by anarchist intellectuals, pushing him towards a new type of dominated culture. This new culture brought together young Jewish intellectuals from Eastern Europe and North Africa; French Israelites were more or less absent.[29] For Bernard Lazare, Zionism was an expression of revolt against the political Left, Israelite culture, traditional republicanism and maybe against "History" as well.

The Left said that anti-Semitism would end with the advent of socialism; Israelites thought that the reign of democratic liberalism would solve the modern Jewish question (Émile Durkheim considered anti-Semitism to be a German export);[30] republicanism invited Jews to blend into the French Republic; Zionism, in both its neo-liberal and socialist poles, raised doubts about these optimistic views, predicting that the contemporary and future upheavals in Europe would contradict the belief in linear, rational progress. The rationalist philosophy of progress concealed irrational currents that were not only remnants of an obscurantist past but fed by the modern masses of democracy.

Bernard Lazare's time with the symbolists may have predisposed him to accepting Zionist thought, making him sensitive to aesthetic expressions of the spiritual metamorphoses of modernity with their unpredictable and irrational manifestations. Symbolism and anarchism heightened his intuition, which was lacking in many other socialists, that irrational elements also participated in the play of signifier and signified in politics.[31] Lazare had a sharper sense that History did not respond to a process of linear universalization that would ensure a free and secure future for the weak and minorities.

The first French Zionist tried desperately, however, to retain some universal values while exploring national specificities. Not only did Bernard Lazare not abandon his libertarianism when joining Zionism, it seems that his vision only grew broader. He increasingly identified with the Jewish proletariat of Central Europe whom he saw as the primary agent of national rebirth. The economic and national oppression suffered by this proletariat made it an ally of international socialism because of its national and universal interest. In a 1900 letter to the president of a circle of Zionist students in Bucharest, he wrote:

> Judaism must be organized everywhere into a proletarian National party. In conquering its freedom, the Jewish people must assert the freedom of its proletariat and lay the foundations for a social republic. In this way, it will serve the cause of the international proletariat at the same time.[32]

Pessimism towards the automatic progression of freedom in the framework of liberalism and socialism gave rise to a different vision in Bernard Lazare, one that partook in a global utopia: the progress of individual freedoms remained connected to the progress of social and economic equality combined with another prerequisite condition, a new dimension: progress for the collective rights of national minorities who join the general struggle for equality.

It is not every day that an anarchist supports the creation of another Nation-State! Bernard Lazare brought resolute support to the idea of creating a State as a haven for the Jews and backed Herzl's colonization project.[33] Lazare fully accepted the notion of political sovereignty as a necessary part of national rebirth; however, the center of gravity of his thinking on the nation concerned the development of a new cultural identity for the ancient Jewish people. From this perspective, he is relatively close to the cultural Zionism of Ahad Ha'am (Asher Ginzberg) and of the Bund, the socialist movement for Jewish autonomy at the start of the century.

The arguments and ruptures between the Jewish communities of Eastern Europe did not reach Bernard Lazare; he saw the creation of the modern Jewish identity within a pluralist framework that would not be limited by a single principle or territory. His anti-Jacobin anarchism made him approach the national question from an original angle compared to the republican culture of the turn of the century: Jewish national identity could just as well lead to emigration to Palestine or staying in place; the modern State could and should integrate different cultural communities that each carry their own national affinities. The tendency to erase intellectual differences between them would be both harmful and even impossible. Political progress does not have to equate to uniqueness or the renunciation of one's cultural personality, the search for unity is moral in character:

> Jews in the world today are a nation without a land. They have a unity that confers on them a nationality; they possess individual traits that it is absolutely legitimate for them to keep. Some reproach them for remaining themselves. As long as they fulfill their duties of human solidarity, how could one refuse them the right to retain their personality? It is an old statist and governmental prejudice that has been passed down into minds that sometimes seem emancipated. The dream of the people who govern is to have subjects who are like children's toy soldiers. Originality and particularities are an anathema to them. In the name of a certain nationalism, they proscribe difference and hope to unify minds and consciences militarily.[34]

At the end of his essay *Job's Dungheap*, published after his death, Bernard Lazare summarized his thoughts on the nation as follows:

> Where is our homeland?—Where have we suffered? Then it is everywhere.... It is made up of so many things, so many memories, regrets, joys, tears and pains that a small parcel of desolate, uncultivated land would not be enough and Jerusalem, like Judea, is only one of the pieces of our homeland.[35]

The national idea must mainly consist of adopting a Jewish self-consciousness, maintaining self-respect and organizing collectively around these ideas. Attempts at assimilation were doomed to fail and fraught with danger. Assimilation, unlike what the socialists claimed, was not a universal act; it was always an attempt at local national fusion requiring Jews to erase the traits of their cultural identity. This process of dilution was not only undesirable but it raised suspicion and ended up contributing to anti-Semitism.

Bernard Lazare, a Dreyfusard and a Zionist, reached the conclusion that persecuted Jews had to assert their Jewish origins and heritage without renouncing their claim to political rights in the countries where they lived:

> Nationalism and emancipation are opposed but by a crude equivocation, emancipation is made into a synonym of assimilation. Emancipation is not assimilation. We want the emancipation of Jews, not their assimilation. Is it not strange to oppose nationalism and emancipation when we want total, integral emancipation, since assimilation will always be disguised slavery... nationalism and emancipation are not contradictory terms; on the contrary, each implies the other

and, for me, the emancipation of the Jews is a necessary prelude to their nationalization.[36]

The progressive point of view of the republican Left saw the political emancipation of the Jews, in the more or less long term, as their national assimilation and the disappearance of their specific traits; according to Bernard Lazare, it represented something that contributed to political anti-Semitism and prejudiced the situation of Jews in the modern State. At the same time, Zionists were mistaken to abandon the struggle for emancipation in favor of equal rights, which conditioned the evolution of the Jewish national consciousness. Jews had to face their oppressors with their heads held high and never hide.

The road to universal freedom and equality is the same as the road to liberty and equality between nations. This principle, which Bernard Lazare adopted as his own, brought him closer to Theodor Herzl's Zionist Congress but also forced him to keep his distance. A movement promoting equality between nations must be based on democratic equality but not in an elitist bourgeois manner. In March 1899, he wrote to Herzl:

> I ask you to accept my resignation as a member of the Zionist Action Committee and to convey my decision to your colleagues. I am no longer able to participate in the work of a committee that has an orientation, practices and actions that I cannot condone. I cannot be a part of an autocratic government that takes as its principle an unacceptable, unjustifiable esotericism. The Action Committee claims to lead the Jewish masses like an ignorant child without inquiring about their needs and aspirations, without considering their economic,

intellectual or moral status. It is an approach that is radically opposed to all of my political and social opinions and I cannot take responsibility for it.[37]

Lazare had no interest in the internal quarrels of the Zionist movement and he personally revered its main leaders, especially Herzl. Yet the fact that the first concern of the Jewish national movement was to start a bank and spend most of its time on secret diplomacy with governments offended his libertarianism; it did not seem capable of raising the national consciousness of the Jews or of changing their image in the eyes of the world.

Bernard Lazare also expressed an even deeper grievance against the Zionist movement. As we know, at the end of the 19th century, it was not common to think about the national question outside of the European context. Lazare had no way of imagining that the colonization movement would face opposition from the local population and that over the years it would also take the form of a national claim and affirmation. But while Lazare could not "think the Palestinians," he could think of the Armenians and of Herzl's support and maneuvering for the Ottoman Sultan when the first massacre of the Armenians finalized his departure from the Zionist movement.

The Zionist Congress gathered in Basel just paid public tribute to Abd-ul-Hamid. The so-called representatives of the oldest of persecuted peoples, those whose history can only be written in blood, sent their greetings to the worst of assassins.... And this people, still bleeding from its wounds, has thrown itself at the feet of a Sultan covered in the blood of others....[38]

One people could not be made free at the expense of another. Herzl's promise to plead the Ottoman cause in Europe seemed catastrophic to Lazare.

His refusal to remain silent in the face of the first massacre of the 20th century led the first French Zionist to participate in the pro-Armenian congress held in Brussels in 1902 (he had stopped participating in Zionist congresses in 1899).[39] Yet he still considered himself to be a Zionist and remained active. He spent the majority of his time assisting Jews in Romania who were under the threat of persecution and segregation.[40] In his last years, Lazare spent most of his energy on atoning for the sins of his youth, helping the same weak Jews that he had castigated in his first writings.

While Lazare no longer agreed with the direction taken by official Zionist policy, he could at least find some consolation in the victory of the Dreyfusards, since he had been the first among them. The Captain's release was encouraging, yet the last article that Lazare published and in which he attacks the Combes cabinet reveals that if he had not died so young, he would have become one of the most incisive critics of triumphant Dreyfusism. He declared without hesitation:

> We have seen how some anti-clerical papers now reproach the defenders of congregations for seeking support from foreign opinion: they recently criticized us for the same thing. Others have requested that the government place the recalcitrant ones who are in revolt against the law in prison: a few years earlier, they were calling for the summary deportation of anyone suspected of anarchism.... If we are not careful, tomorrow, they will require us to applaud the French gendarmes who take children by the arm to force them to attend a secular school....[41]

It is not by chance that during the last year of his life, he found his way to Péguy's boutique, a gathering place for those disappointed by Dreyfusism.[42]

In our century where so many intellectuals have cast a blind eye on certain injustices in order to denounce others and where one crime can hide another, it may be worthwhile to remember this Jewish intellectual from the end of the 19th century who quickly understood that yesterday's victim could become today's tormentor. He saw that all complacency towards injustice should be rejected, even when the injustices are committed by victims. This intellectual asked us to refuse any compromise with those who persecute others, even if they wave the same flag and he urged us not to turn our backs on the oppressed even if we think they are very different from us. It made him a stubborn anarchist, an intolerable Dreyfusard, an odd Zionist and it may explain why he is still not a saint, a hero or a prophet.

Notes

Preface: Where I Am Speaking From

1. Part of this work was published. See "Jean Jaurès et la question nationale," *Pluriel-débat*, XII, 1977, p. 31–52.

2. This talk was published in Isaiah Berlin, *Against the Current: Essays in the History of Ideas*, New York, Viking, 1980.

3. See for example Antonio Gramsci, *Selections from Political Writings 1910–1920*, Minneapolis, University of Minnesota Press, 1990.

4. François Furet, *The Passing of an Illusion: The Idea of Communism in the Twentieth Century*, Chicago, University of Chicago Press, 1995.

5. See *L'Illusion du politique. Georges Sorel et le débat intellectuel 1900* [The Political Illusion. Georges Sorel and Intellectual Debate in 1900], Paris, La Découverte, 1984.

6. See Jacques Julliard and Shlomo Sand (dir.), *Georges Sorel en son temps* [Georges Sorel in His Time], Paris, Seuil, 1985.

7. I have published a book on these subjects: *Intellectuals, Truth and Power: From the Dreyfus Affair to the Gulf War* (in Hebrew), Tel Aviv, Am Oved, 2000. See also my articles "Mirror, Mirror on the Wall, Who is the True Intellectual of Them All? Self-Image of the Intellectual in France," in Jeremy Jennings (dir.), *Intellectuals in Twentieth-Century France*, London, Macmillan, 1993, p. 33–58; "Le marxisme et les intellectuels vers 1900" [Marxism and Intellectuals around 1900] in Madeleine Réberioux and Gilles Candar (dir.), *Jaurès et les intellectuels* [Jaurès and Intellectuals], Paris, L'Atelier, 1994, p. 203–222; and "A Flirt or a Love Affair? French Intellectuals between Fascism and Nazism," in Edward J. Arnold (dir.), *The Development of the Radical Right in France*, London, Macmillan, 2000, p. 83–99.

8. See *Film as History—Imagining and Screening the Twentieth Century* (in Hebrew), Tel Aviv, Am Oved & Open University Press, 2002.

Introduction: Intellectuals and the National Imagination

1. Régis Debray, *Le Pouvoir intellectuel en France* [Intellectual Power in France], Paris, Ramsay, 1979; Jacques Julliard and Michel Winock, *Dictionnaire des intellectuels français* [Dictionary of French Intellectuals], Paris, Seuil, 1996.

2. Julien Benda, *The Treason of the Intellectuals (La Trahison des clercs)*, Piscataway, NJ, Transaction Publishers, 2006; Raymond Aron, *The Opium of the Intellectuals*, Piscataway, NJ, Transaction Publishers, 2001; Jean-Paul Sartre, *Plaidoyer pour les intellectuels* [In Defense of Intellectuals], Paris, Gallimard, 1972.

3. Lewis A. Coser, *Men of Ideas*, New York, Simon & Shuster, 1965; György Konrád and Iván Szelényi, *The Intellectuals on the Road to Class Power*, Sussex, Harvester Press, 1979; and Russell Jacoby, *The Last Intellectuals*, New York, Noonday Press, 1989.

4. Marc Bloch, *Feudal Society: Vol 2: Social Classes and Political Organization*, New York, Routledge, 1961, p. 160.

5. Benedict Anderson, *Imagined Communities: Reflections on the Origin and Spread of Nationalism*, New York, Verso, 1983; Ernest Gellner, *Nations and Nationalism*, Ithaca, NY, Cornell University Press, 1983; Eric Hobsbawm, *Nations and Nationalism since 1780: Programme, Myth, Reality*, Cambridge, Cambridge University Press, 1990.

6. Alexander Motyl (dir.), *Encyclopedia of Nationalism*, London, Academic Press, 2000.

7. See for example Edward Shils, "The Intellectuals in the Political Development of the New States," *World Politics*, XII, 3, 1960, p. 329–368, and Toyin Falola, *Nationalism and African Intellectuals*, New York, University of Rochester Press, 2001.

8. Michael Keren's short book, *The Pen and the Sword. Israeli Intellectuals and the Making of a Nation-State*, Boulder, Westview Press, 1989, is an exception.

9. Theodor Herzl, *The Jewish State*, Mineola, NY, Dover Publications, 1989.

10. Ernst Pawel, *Labyrinth of Exile: A Life of Theodor Herzl*, New York, Farrar, Strauss & Giroux, 1989. In his journal, Herzl wrote: "I owe much to Drumont for my present freedom of conception, because he is an artist." (*ibid.*)

11. Christophe Charle, "Champ littéraire et champ du pouvoir: les écrivains et l'affaire Dreyfus" [Literature and Power: Writers and the Dreyfus Affair], *Annales*,

XXXII, 2, 1977, p. 240–264, and Jean-Denis Bredin, *L'Affaire*, Paris, Julliard, 1983. See also Pierre Vidal-Naquet, "Dreyfus dans l'Affaire et dans l'histoire" [Dreyfus in the Affair and in History], in *Les Juifs, la mémoire et le présent* [The Jews, Memory and the Present], vol. II Paris, La Découverte, 1991, p. 88–128.

12. From the accelerated and traumatic industrialization that contributed to the particular hunger of the *Gemeinschaft* in Germany to demographic decline in France which had some influence on the civic openness that is characteristic of the French national identity, the historical complexity at the basis of the development of any national imagination is a subject that I will not be able to broach in this brief introduction.

13. Émile Durkheim, *La Science sociale et l'action*, Paris, PUF, 1970, p. 269–270.

14. See for example Léon Blum's book, *Souvenirs sur l'Affaire* [Memories of the Affair], Paris, Gallimard,1935 and the article by Annie Kriegel, "Aux origines françaises du sionisme: l'affaire Dreyfus" [The French Origins of Zionism: the Dreyfus Affair] in *Les Juifs et le monde moderne* [Jews and the Modern World], Paris, Seuil, 1977, p. 167–179.

15. See my article, "Bernard Lazare, le premier sioniste français" [Bernard Lazare, the First French Zionist], *Revue française d'histoire des idées politiques*, 4, 1996, p. 281–296. On the attitude of Jewish community organizations towards Zionism, see Michael R. Marrs, *Les Juifs à l'époque de l'affaire Dreyfus* [Jews at the time of the Dreyfus Affair], Paris, Calmann-lévy, 1972, p. 279–321. For another opinion, see Pierre Birnbaum, "La citoyenneté en péril: les juifs entre intégration et résistance" [Citizenship in Peril: Jews between Integration and Resistance], in Pierre Birnbaum (dir.), *La France de l'affaire Dreyfus*, Paris, Gallimard, 1994, p. 505–542.

16. Moritz Lazarus, a professor of philosophy and psychology at the University of Berlin and a reformed Jew, also participated in the debate with Treitschke. In 1879, he gave a conference with the title "Was heisst 'national'?" ("What does 'national' mean?") that was reminiscent of the principles Ernest Renan had presented in his talk "Qu'est-ce qu'une nation?" ("What is a Nation?") published three years later. On the debate with Treitschke, see Reuven Michael, *Heinrich Graetz. The Historian of the Jewish People* (in Hebrew), Jerusalem, Bialik, 2003, p. 161–179. (The titles of articles and books in Hebrew are given in the English translation that they were given when published.)

1. "People of the Book" and People of Letters

1. On Max Nordau, see Delphine Bechtel, Dominique Bourel and Jacques Le Rider (dir.), *Max Nordau, 1849–1923*, Paris: Cerf, 1996.

2. See Ernest Gellner, *Nations and Nationalism, op. cit.*

3. See Edward Shils, *The Intellectuals and the Powers and Other Essays*, Chicago, University of Chicago Press, 1972.

4. The General Jewish Labor Bund of Lithuania, Poland and Russia, more commonly known as "The Bund," was a Jewish socialist party founded in 1897 in the Russian Empire. On the Bund in Russia, see Nathan Weinstock, *Le Pain de la misère. Histoire du mouvement ouvrier juif en Europe* [Bread of Misery. History of the Jewish Labor Movement in Europe], vol. 1, Paris, La Découverte, 1984, and Henri Minczeles, *Histoire générale du Bund, un mouvement révolutionnaire juif* [General History of the Bund, a Jewish Revolutionary Movement], Paris, Denoël, 1999.

5. Born in Russia in 1879, Vladimir Medem was one of the leading theorists of the Bund. He defended its autonomy in the Russian social democracy, which led to several clashes with Lenin. In 1917, he opposed the Bolsheviks' seizure of power. He emigrated to New York and died there in 1923. See his autobiography *Fun mayn Lebn*, New York, Vladimir Medem Komite, 1923.

6. Otto Bauer (1881–1935) was one of the leaders of the Austrian Social Democrats from their founding until Hitler took power. He is primarily known for his work on the national question and was strongly criticized by Lenin before 1914. See his book *The Question of Nationalities and Social Democracy*, Minneapolis, University of Minnesota Press, 2000.

7. On the development of Hebrew culture in Russia, see Dan Miron, *When Loners Come Together. A Portrait of Hebrew Literature at the Turn of the Twentieth Century* (in Hebrew), Tel Aviv, Am Oved, 1970.

8. Yosef Gorny, "The Changes in the Social and the Political Structure of the 'Second Aliyah' in the Years 1904–1940" (in Hebrew), *Zionut*, I, 1970, p. 205–246.

9. For more on this exceptional figure, see Eliezer Schweid, *The World of A.D. Gordon* (in Hebrew), Tel Aviv, Am Oved, 1970.

10. On the social profile of cultural elites between 1918 and 1948, see Moshe Lissak, *The Elites of the Jewish Community in Palestine* (in Hebrew), Tel Aviv, Am Oved, 1981, p. 93–96, 156–159, 172–175.

11. See for example Avraham Cordova, "Unsollicited Intellectuals in Politics: the Case of Brit Ha-Biryonim," in Pinhas Ginossar (dir.), *Hebrew Literature and the Labor Movement* (in Hebrew), Beer Sheva, Ben-Gurion University Press, 1989, p. 224–242.

12. On the development of the "Israeli language," see Itamar Even Zohar, "The Emergence of a Native Hebrew Culture in Palestine 1882–1948," *Studies in Zion-*

ism IV, 1981, p. 167–184, and Paul Wexler, *The Schizoid Nature of Modern Hebrew: a Slavic Language in Search of a Semitic Past*, Wiesbaden, Otto Harrassowitz, 1991.

13. In 1921, Bialik moved to Germany, living first in Hamburg and then in Berlin, where he founded the Dvir publishing house, which later became a leading Israeli publisher. On this subject, see Zohar Shavit, *The Literary Life in Eretz Israel 1910–1933* (in Hebrew), Tel Aviv, Ha-Kibutz Ha-Meuchad, 1982.

14. See Avraham Cordova, "The Institutionalization of a Cultural Center in Palestine: the Writers' Association," *Jewish Social Studies*, XLII, 1, 1980, p. 37–62.s

15. See Avraham Cordoba and Hanna Herzog, "The Cultural Endeavor of the Labor Movement in Palestine: a Study of the Relationship between Intelligentsia and Intellectuals," *Yivo, Annual of Jewish Social Science*, VII, 1978, p. 241–242.

16. See Nurith Gertz, *Literature and Ideology in Eretz Israel during the 1930s* (in Hebrew), Tel Aviv, The Open University Press, 1988.

17. The major Palestinian revolt against British and Zionist colonization erupted in 1936. It was quickly successful in rural regions, where groups of solidly armed and organized farmers attacked communications routes and Jewish settlements. In the main cities, the insurgents were briefly able to take control of the central neighborhoods. The revolt continued until 1939.

18. On the relationship between the teacher's union and the political elite, see Moshe Rinot, "The Struggle between the Teacher's Union and the Zionist Organization for Hegemony in Hebrew Education in Palestine" (in Hebrew), *Zionut*, IV, 1975, p. 114–145, and Yonathan Shapira, *An Elite without Successors. Generations of Political Leaders in Israel* (in Hebrew), Tel Aviv, Sifriat Poalim, 1984, p. 66–92.

19. See Uri Cohen, *Intellectuals in a National Crystallization Process. The Relationship of the Hebrew University in Jerusalem and the Jewish Settlement in Eretz-Israel, 1925–1948* (in Hebrew, unpublished Master's thesis), Hebrew University of Jerusalem, 1996.

20. Paul R. Mendes-Flohr (dir.), *A Land of Two Peoples. Martin Buber on Jews and Arabs*, New York, Oxford University Press, 1983, p. 74. See also Aaron Kedar, "Brith Shalom: documents and introduction," *The Jerusalem Quarterly*, XVIII, 1981, p. 55–85.

21. Hagit Lavsky, "The Puzzle of Brith Shalom's Impact on the Zionist Polemic during its time and afterwards" (in Hebrew), *Zionut*, XIX, 1995, p. 167–181. See also Joseph Heller, *From Brith Shalom to Ichud. Judah Leib Magnes and the Struggle for a Binational State in Palestine* (in Hebrew), Jerusalem, Magnes, 2003.

22. For more on the Canaanites, see the book by James Diamond, *Homeland or Holy Land: The "Canaanite" Critique of Israel*, Indianapolis, Indiana University Press, 1986.

23. The first Israeli-Arab conflict broke out the day after the declaration of independence of the Hebrew State on May 14, 1948. On the morning of May 15, the armies of Transjordan, Egypt and Syria entered Palestine, along with Libyan and Iraqi contingents. This war established the independence of the State of Israel and divided the remaining land from the British mandate between Egypt and Transjordan.

24. See Dan Miron, "From Creators and Builders to Homeless" (in Hebrew), *Igra. Almanac for Literature and Art*, II, 1985–1986, p. 106–118.

25. On this subject, see Michael Keren, *Ben-Gurion and the Intellectuals. Power, Knowledge and Charisma*, Illinois, Northern Illinois University Press, 1983.

26. Shmuel N. Eisenstadt, *Israeli Society, Background, Development and Problems* (in Hebrew), Jerusalem, Magnes, 1967, p. 331.

27. On the development of universities, see Joseph Ben David, "Universities in Israel: dilemmas of growth, diversification and administration" in E. Krausz (dir.), *Education, in a Comparative Context. Studies of Israeli Society*, IV, New Brunswick, Transaction Publishers, 1989, p. 148–173.

28. On the number of students at the end of the 1950s, see Shmuel N. Eisenstadt, *The Transformation of Israeli Society* (in Hebrew), Jerusalem, Magnes, 1989, p. 297.

29. Accused of ordering a series of aggressive anti-British attacks in Egypt (1954–55)—attacks that failed to have any victims but cost the lives of several Israeli agents—Pinhas Lavon, the minister who had "inherited" the Defense portfolio from Ben-Gurion, was forced to resign.

30. The 1967 War, also called the "Six-Day War" because of the number of days of military operations in the strict sense, was the third armed conflict between Israel and its neighbors. While it ended in a solid victory for the Israeli army, it also led to a profound modification of its borders. With the occupation of East Jerusalem, the West Bank, Gaza, the Golan Heights and Sinai, the Hebrew State quadrupled the size of its territory.

31. See Dan Miron, "Document in Israel" (in Hebrew), *Politika*, August 16, 1987, p. 37–45.

32. See Michael Feige, *One Space, Two Places: "Gush Emunim," "Peace Now" and the Construction of Israeli Space* (in Hebrew), Jerusalem, Magnes, 2002.

33. See Tamar Herman, *From the "Peace Covenant" to "Peace Now": the Pragmatic Pacifism of the Israeli Peace Camp* (in Hebrew, unpublished doctoral thesis), Tel Aviv University, 1989, p. 258–297.

34. On June 6, 1982, the Israeli army launched "Operation Peace for Galilee" against the Palestinian presence in Lebanon. It invaded Lebanon and placed Beirut under siege. Defeated, the Palestine Liberation Organization (PLO) left Lebanon for Tunisia. Israeli troops pulled out of Lebanon in 1985 while maintaining a "security zone" in the south of the country until May 2000.

35. On this subject, see Ella Shohat, *Israeli Cinema, East/West and the Politics of Representation*, Austin, University of Texas Press, 1989, p. 237–273.

36. The first Oslo Accords (September 13, 1993) were signed in Washington. Present at the signing were Yitzhak Rabin, Israeli Prime Minister, Yasser Arafat, President of the PLO Executive Committee, and Bill Clinton, President of the United States.

37. Popular novelist David Grossman's positions on the territories were an exception. At the end of 1987, he published a striking tale of his visits to the West Bank. See *The Yellow Wind*, New York, Picador, 2002.

38. On the diverse fallout of the Palestinian Intifada on political culture in Israel, see Reuven Gal (dir.), *The Seventh War. The Effects of the Intifada on the Israeli Society* (in Hebrew), Tel Aviv, Ha-Kibutz Ha-Meuchad, 1990.

39. See Yona Hadar-Ramage (dir.), *Thinking It Over. Conflicts in Israeli Public Thought* (in Hebrew), Ramat Efal, Yad Tabenkin, 1994, p. 695.

40. For a slightly different analysis of Israeli intellectuals during this period, see the short book by Bruce Maddy-Weitzman, *Palestinian and Israeli Intellectuals in the Shadow of Oslo and Intifadat Al-Aqsa*, Tel Aviv, Dayan Center, 2003. On Rabin's assassination, see also Amnon Kapeliouk, *Rabin—un assassinat politique*, Paris, Le Monde Éditions, 1996.

41. See the interesting, albeit overly apologetic book by Menahem Klein, *Bar-Ilan. University between Religion and Politics*, (in Hebrew), Jerusalem, Magnes, 1998.

42. See Yoram Hazoni, *The Jewish State: the Struggle for Israel's Soul*, New York, Basic Books, 2001.

43. See for example Irena Vrubel-Golubkina and Nir Baram (dir.), *Contemporary Russian Literature in Israeli Discourse* (in Hebrew), Tel Aviv, Am Oved, 2005.

44. See his excellent book, Yehouda Shenav, *The Arab-Jew. Nationalism, Religion and Ethnicity* (in Hebrew), Tel Aviv, Am Oved, 2003.

45. The following pages deal with a period when the author was personally engaged in the political debates of the intellectual sphere. His involvement is apparent in his writing.

46. See Anton Shammas, *Arabesques*, Berkeley, University of California Press, 2001, a semi-autobiographic novel written in Hebrew.

47. See Azmi Bishara, *The Arabs in Israel*, Gloucestershire, Arris Books, 2003, et id., *Checkpoint*, Arles, Actes Sud, 2004.

48. See *Yediot Hahronot*, December 31, 1999 and January 5, 2000, and *Haaretz*, January 6, 2000.

49. On the position of Ehud Yaari and his influence on electronic media, see *Haaretz*, November 10, 2000.

50. *New York Times*, July 28, 2000. On Amos Oz's positions during Camp David and afterwards, see his collection of articles *But These are Two Different Wars* (in Hebrew), Tel Aviv, Keter, 2002.

51. These quotes are taken from a collection of interviews on the erratic behavior of intellectuals that appeared in *Haaretz*, October 20, 2005. On this crisis, see also Yitzhak Laor, *Things that are better (Not) Kept Silent—Essays* (in Hebrew), Tel-Aviv, Babel, 2002, p. 78–108.

52. See Benny Morris, *The Birth of the Palestinian Refugee Problem, 1947–1949*, Cambridge, Cambridge University Press, 1988.

53. See *Yediot Hahronot*, November 23, 2001, and *Haaretz*, January 9, 2004.

54. See *Haaretz* and *Yediot Hahronot*, Spetember 26, 2003.

55. On disobedience in Israel, see Peretz Kidron (dir.), *Refuznik! Les soldats de la conscience en Israël*, Villeurbanne, Golias, 2005.

56. On the intellectuals who supported the pilots' petition, see *Haaretz*, October 10, 2003.

57. See his interview in *Haaretz*, October 8, 2004.

58. On the position of prominent intellectuals on the retreat from Gaza, see the articles collected by Ari Shavit (dir.), *Partition, Disengagement and Beyond* (in Hebrew), Tel Aviv, Keter, 2005.

59. On this contradiction, see for example Oren Yiftachel, "Ethnocracy: the Politics of Judaizing Israel/Palestine" *Constellation*, 6, 1999, p. 364–390. See also Baruch Kimmerling, *The Invention and Decline of Israelness. State, Society and the Military*, Berkeley, University of California Press, 2001, p. 173–207. See also Alain Gresh, *Israël-Palestine, vérités sur un conflit*, Fayard, Paris, 2001, p. 158–162. [Israel, Palestine, truths about a conflict.]

2. Words That Think Through Us

1. On the importance of words in various linguistic structures, see for example, Gareth Stedman Jones, *Languages of Class: Studies in English Working-Class History, 1832–1982*, Cambridge, Cambridge University Press, 1983, and Reinhart Koselleck, *Futures Past: On the Semantics of Historical Time*, Cambridge, MIT Press, 1990.

2. On the semantics of the idea of nation, see the excellent collection by Sylvianne Rémi-Giraud and Pierre Rétat (dir.) *Les Mots de la nation* [Words of the Nation] Lyon, Presses Universitaires de Lyon, 1996, and Gérard Noiriel, "Socio-histoire d'un concept: les usages du mot 'nationalité' au 19e siècle" [Sociohistory of a Concept: the Use of the Word Nationality in the 19th century] in *État, nation et immigration*, Paris, 2005, p. 219–247.

3. The translation of *Galut* or *Gola* is not "diaspora" as often thought. "Diaspora" in Hebrew is *Pzura*.

4. See on this subject the collection by James M. Scott (ed.), *Exile: Old Testament, Jewish and Christian Conceptions*, Leyden, Brill, 1997.

5. Shmuel Almog, *Nationalism Zionism, Antisemitism* (in Hebrew), Jerusalem, Ha-Sifria, Ha-Ziyonit, 1992, p. 67.

6. Moses Hess, *Rome and Jerusalem*, Charleston, SC, Nabu Press, 2010.

7. When the autonomists spoke of the Jewish people, they meant the Yiddish people living in the settlement zones of the Russian Empire, in Galicia and Romania, or the territories that were once part of Greater Poland. The theorists of the Bund party, for example, had no difficulty in proving that those who spoke Yiddish in Eastern Europe, unlike the vestiges of Jewish communities in Western Europe or the communities practicing the Jewish religion in Islamic countries, had a specific religious tradition but also a flourishing secular popular culture that distinguished them entirely from the cultures and languages of neighboring peoples.

8. Vladimir Jabotinsky, "The Race," in *Exile and Assimilation* (in Hebrew), Tel-Aviv, Saltzman, 1936, p. 292.

9. Ber Borochov, *Works*, vol. I (in Hebrew), Tel-Aviv, Ha-Kibutz Ha-Meuchad, 1955, p. 148.

10. Max Nordau, "The History of the Israeli People" (1901, in Hebrew), in *Zionist Works*, vol. II, Jerusalem, Ha-Sifria Ha-Ziyonit, 1960, p. 47. See also the interview he gave with Édouard Drumont's paper, *La Libre Parole*, December 21, 1903. Arthur Ruppin, *The Social Structure of the Jews* (in Hebrew), Berlin/Tel-Aviv, Shtibel, 1934, p. 15. The chapters in this book are titled "The racial Composition of the Jews of Israel" and "The History of the Race of the Jews outside Israel." The author admits in the introduction that the theory of the Jewish race preoccupied him for dozens of years. At the end of the work, there are several pictures of characteristic "Jewish" faces in different communities presented to confirm his main theses.

11. Assa Kasher, "Zionism 2000—Fundamental assumptions and guiding principles," in Pinhas Ginossar and Avi Bareli (dir.), *Zionism. A Contemporary Controversy. Research Trends and Ideological Approaches* (in Hebrew). Beer Sheva, Ben-Gurion University Press, 1996, p. 511.

12. Yaacov Shavit, "Nationalism, Historiography and Historical Revision" (in Hebrew), in Pinhas Ginossar and Avi Barelli (dir.), *Zionism. A Contemporary Controversy, op. cit.*, p. 272.

13. Aviva Halamish, "Zionist Immigration Policy in the 1930s: from 'Redemption' to 'Survival'" (in Hebrew), *Zmanim*, XIV, 58, 1997, p. 86–98.

14. Yehoshua Porath, *The Emergence of the Palestinian-Arab National Movement*, New York, Routledge, 1995.

15. Ya'acov Barnai, *Historiography and Nationalism* (in Hebrew), Jerusalem, Magnes, 1995, p. 87. For an analysis of the relationship between Jews and the "Land of Israel" and the justifications for using this expression (before the 1967 War) see R.J. Zwi Werblowsky, "Israël et Eretz Israël," *Les Temps modernes*, 253 bis, 1967, p. 317–393, and Shmuel Ettinger, "Le peuple juif et Eretz Israël," *ibid.*, p. 394–413. On this subject, see also Jean-Christophe Attias and Esther Benbassa, *Israël imaginaire*, Paris, Flammarion, 1998.

16. Leon Pinsker, *Auto-Emancipation*, New York, The Maccabaean Publishing Co., 1906, p. 11.

17. In 1903, British minister Joseph Chamberlain proposed that Herzl create a Jewish state in Uganda, which was under British rule at the time. Herzl, fearing that the chance for Palestine was lost, wanted to accept the offer quickly and organized the 6th Zionist Congress in Basel. The delegates refused to accept anything other than Palestine. At the end of the Congress, however, a majority was ready to accept the British offer.

18. David Ben-Gurion and Yitzhak Ben Zvi, *Eretz Israel in the Past and the Present* (in Hebrew), Jerusalem, Yad Ben Zvi, 1979, p. 46.

19. Vladimir Jabotinsky, "The Iron Wall," in *The Road to a State* (in Hebrew), Jerusalem, Ari Jabotinsky, 1963, p. 255.

20. See Benedict Anderson, *Imagined Communities, op. cit.*

21. Amoz Oz, *In the Land of Israel*, New York, Mariner Books, 1993.

22. On April 6, 1903, in Kishinev, the bloodiest pogrom of the history of the Russian Empire took place. Over two days, a violent mob killed, injured, raped and looted. 49 people died, 100 were injured and a thousand homes were destroyed.

23. I will not refer here to the stages in which European colonialism committed mass systematic massacres on subjugated populations. One example is Africa, where millions of people were killed.

24. Marc Ferro used a similar approach in his book *Comment on raconte l'histoire aux enfants à travers le monde entier* [How History is Told to Children around the World], Paris, Payot, 1983.

3. "Analogical" Intellectuals and the Gulf War

1. See *Hayer*, March 1, 1991, p. 30–32.

2. See *Haaretz*, February 14, 1991.

3. See *Al Hamishmar*, January 25, 1991.

4. *Haaretz*, February 7, 1991.

5. *Haaretz*, February 1 and 15, 1991. Reprinted in Nathan Shaham and Zvi Raanan (dir.), *War in the Gulf. Collection of Essays* (in Hebrew), Tel Aviv, Sifriat Poalim, 1991, p. 9–21.

6. *Ibid.*, p. 12–13.

7. *Ibid.*, p. 14.

8. *Ibid.*, p. 16.

9. See *Al Hamishmar*, January 29, 1991; *Haaretz*, January 29, 1991; and *Hadashot*, February 1, 1991.

10. *Al Hamishmar*, February 5, 1991.

11. An Israeli city in the Negev desert.

12. See *Iton Tel Aviv*, March 29, 1991. On Yoram Kaniuk and Günter Grass, see also Moshe Zuckermann, *Shoah and the Sealed Room. The "Holocaust" in Israeli Press During the Gulf War* (in Hebrew), Tel Aviv, private edition, 1993, p. 289–302.

13. *Yediot Hahronot*, January 27, 1991.

14. *Maariv*, January 24, 1991.

15. *Haaretz*, January 25, 1991.

16. *Yediot Hahronot*, January 24, 1991.

17. *Hadashot*, February 1, 1991.

18. *Yediot Hahronot*, January 25 and February 1, 1991.

19. See *Haaretz*, June 25, 1993.

20. *Haaretz*, January 18, 1991; *Yediot Hahronot*, February 7, 1991; *Al Hamishmar*, February 7, 1991; *Maariv*, February 8, 1991; *Hadashot*, February 8, 1991.

4. Post-Zionism: A Historiographical or Intellectual Debate?

1. Simha Flapan, *The Birth of Israel: Myths and realities*, New York, Pantheon, 1987; Avi Shlaim, *Collusion Across the Jordan: King Abdullah, the Zionist Movement and the Partition of Palestine*, Oxford, Oxford University Press, 1988; Ilan Pappé, *Britain and the Arab-Israeli Conflict, 1948–1951*, London, Macmillan, 1988; Benny Morris, *The Birth of the Palestinian refugee Problem, 1947–1949*, op. cit.; Boaz Evron, *A National Reckoning* (in Hebrew), Tel-Aviv, Dvir, 1988; Gershon Shafir, *Land, Labor and the Origins of the Israeli-Palestinian Conflict, 1882–1914*,

Cambridge, Cambridge University Press, 1989. On the start of the polemic, see Benny Morris, "The New Historiography: Israel Confronts its Past," *Tikkun*, IV, 1988, p. 19–23 and 99–102. There is an attempted synthesis in Laurence J. Silberstein, *The Postzionism Debates. Knowledge and Power in Israeli Culture*, New York, Routledge, 1999. See also in French the book by Ilan Greilsammer, *La Nouvelle histoire d'Israël. Essai sur une identité nationale* [The New History of Israel. Essay on a National Identity], Paris, Gallimard, 1998.

2. See, for example, the two books by members of the Matzpen: A. Lisraeli (Akiva Orr and Moshe Machover), *Peace, Peace, When There Is No Peace* (in Hebrew), Jerusalem, Bokhan, 1961; Arie Bober (dir.), *The Other Israel: The Radical Case against Zionism*, New York, Doubleday Anchor, 1972; as well as the work by Israel Berr, *Israel's Security: Yesterday, Today, Tomorrow* (in Hebrew), Tel Aviv, Amikam, 1966; and the essay by Uri Avneri, *Israel Without Zionists*, London, Macmillan, 1968.

3. See Ariel Rein, "History and Jewish History: Together or Separate? The Definition of Historical Studies at the Hebrew University, 1925–1935," in Shaul Katz and Michael Heyd (dir.), *The History of the Hebrew University of Jerusalem. Origins and Beginnings* (in Hebrew), Jerusalem, Magnes, 1997, p. 516–540.

4. Yitzhak Baer, *Galut*, New York, Schoken Books, 1947, p. 120.

5. The Ben-Gurion University of Beer Sheva, a relatively new university, is the only one that has a single History department. But the different options are compartmentalized and history studies are currently being separated into two departments.

6. On this subject, see the previous chapter.

7. See, for example, Ilan Pappé, "Critique and Agenda: Post-Zionist Scholars in Israel," *History and Memory*, VII, 1, 1995, p. 66–90.

8. To this encouraging theoretical discourse, we should also add the book by Edward Saïd, *Orientalism*, (New York, Vintage Books, 1979), and the important polemic that followed it at the end of the 1970s. See Gabriel Piterberg, "The Nation and its Raconteurs: *Orientalism* and Nationalist Historiography" (In Hebrew), *Theory and Criticism*, VI, 1995, p. 81–103.

9. Simha Flapan had been a long-standing member of the United Workers Party (Mapam) and editor of the review *New Outlook*. After his death in 1987, his book was published in Hebrew by his wife; it appeared in 1990 in a private edition.

10. Ilan Pappé's works are available in English, including *The Making of the Arab-Israeli Conflict, 1947–1951*, New York, I.B. Tauris, 1992 and *The Modern History*

of Palestine, One Land, Two Peoples, Cambridge Cambridge University Press, 2003. See also Eugene L. Rogan and Avi Shlaim (dir.), *The War for Palestine: Rewriting the History of 1948*, Cambridge, Cambridge University Press, 2001. We could add to the list of publications that have called into question the traditional positions on the 1948 war Yoram Nimrod's important book, *War or Peace? Formation of Patterns in Israeli Arab Relations, 1947–1950* (in Hebrew), Givat Haviva, Institute for Peace Studies, 2000.

11. Benny Morris proposed the idea of a transfer in his collection of articles *Correcting a Mistake: Jews and Arabs in Palestine/Israel, 1936–1956* (in Hebrew), Tel-Aviv, Am Oved, 2000. See also his book *The Birth of the Palestinian Refugee Problem Revisited*, Cambridge University Press, 2004.

12. See for example Anita Shapira, "Politicians and Collective Memory: the Debate over the New Historians in Israel," *History and Memory*, VII, 1, 1995, p. 9–40; Moshe Lissak, "'Critical' Sociologists and 'Establishment' Sociologists in the Israeli Academic Community: Ideological Struggles or an Academic Discourse?," *Israel Studies*, I, 1, 1996, p. 247–294; Pinhas Ginossar and Avi Bareli (dir.), *Zionism. A Contemporary Controversy, op. cit.*; Yechiam Weitz (dir.), *From Vision to Revision. A Hundred Years of Historiography of Zionism* (in Hebrew), Jerusalem, Zalman Shazar, 1997; Efraim Karsh, *Fabricating Israeli History: "The New Historians,"* London, Frank Cass, 1997; Anita Shapira and Derek J. Penslar (dir.), *Israeli Historical Revisionism: From Left to Right*, London, Frank Cass, 2002; and Tuvia Friling (dir.), *Critique du post-sionisme: réponse aux "nouveaux historiens" israéliens*, Paris, In Press, 2004.

13. Tom Segev, *The Seventh Million: The Israelis and the Holocaust*, New York, Hill & Wang, 1994.

14. Shabtai Beit Zvi, *Post-Uganda Zionism in the Crisis of the Shoah* (in Hebrew), Tel Aviv, Bronfman, 1977.

15. Yosef Grodzinsky, *Good Human Material* (in Hebrew), Or Yehuda, Hed Arzi Publishing, 1998 (in English: *In the Shadow of the Holocaust: The Struggle between Jews and Zionists in the Aftermath of World War II*, Monroe, Common Courage Press, 2004). See also Idith Zertal, *From Catastrophe to Power: The Holocaust Survivors and the Emergence of Israel*, Berkeley, University of California Press, 1998.

16. Bruce Kimmerling (dir.), *The Israeli State and Society: Boundaries and Frontiers*, Albany, State University of New York Press, 1989.

17. Baruch Kimmerling and Joel Migdal, *Palestinians: The Making of a People*, New York, The Free Press, 1993 (the book also appeared in Hebrew in 1999).

18. See for example Baruch Kimmerling, "Academic History Caught in the Cross-fire: The Case of Israeli-Jewish Historiography," *History and Memory*, VII, 1, 1995, p. 41–65, as well as *The Invention and Decline of Israeliness, op. cit.*, and *Immigrants, Settlers, Natives. The Israeli State and Society between Cultural Pluralism and Cultural Wars* (in Hebrew), Tel Aviv, AM Oved, 2004.

19. Uri Ram, "Zionist Historiography and the Invention of Modern Jewish Nation-hood: The Case of Ben Zion Dinur," *History and Memory*, VII, 1, 1995, p. 91–124. On the development of historiography at the Hebrew University of Jerusalem, see also David N. Myers, *Re-Inventing the Jewish Past: European Jewish Intellectuals and Zionist Return to History*, New York, Oxford University Press, 1995.

20. On this subject, see the article by Zeev Herzog in *Haaretz*, October 29, 1999; Diana V. Edelman (dir.), *The Triumph of Elohim from Yahwism to Judaism*, Michigan, William B. Eerdmans, 1996; and Israel Finkelstein and Neil Asher Silberman, *The Bible Unearthed: Archaeology's New Vision of Ancient Israel and the Origin of Its Sacred Texts*, New York, The Free Press, 2001.

21. The only doctoral thesis that took up part of the "post-Zionist" theme, and is sadly unpublished, is Amnon Raz-Krakotzkin, *The National Narration of Exile. Zionist Historiography and Medieval Jewry* (in Hebrew, unpublished doctoral thesis), University of Tel Aviv, 1996.

22. On this subject, see also Chapter 2.

Epilogue: Bernard Lazare, the First French Zionist

1. For many years, the only ones who published Bernard Lazare belonged to a certain nationalist Right with the Librairie française and a wing of the radical Left in the Éditions de la Différence. On this point, see: Pierre Vidal-Naquet, "Sur une réédition," in *Les Juifs, la mémoire et le présent*, Vol. II, Paris, La Découverte, 1991, p. 85–87.

2. After years of indifference and forgetting, Bernard Lazare's works have made a timid reappearance over the past five years as articles and essays that shed better light on his ideas. See *Le Fumier de Job* [Job's Dungheap], Strasbourg, Ciré, 1990; *Juifs & antisémites* [Jews & Antisemites], (edited by Philippe Oriol), Paris, Éditions Allia, 1992, and *Une erreur judiciaire, l'affaire Dreyfus* [A Miscarriage of Justice, the Dreyfus Affair], Paris, Éditions Allia, 1993.

3. Cf. Nelly Wilson, *Bernard-Lazare*, Paris, Albin Michel, 1985. See also Jean-Denis Bredin's compelling book, *Bernard Lazare. De l'anarchiste au prophète* [Bernard Lazare. From Anarchist to Prophet], Paris, Éditions de Fallois, 1992.

4. See especially *La Porte d'ivoire* [The Ivory Door] and *Les Porteurs de torche* [The Torch Bearers], Paris, Armand Colin, 1897 as well as his essays *Figures contemporaines, ceux d'aujourd'hui, ceux de demain* [Contemporary Figures of Today and Tomorrow], Paris, Perrin, 1895, and *L'Écrivain et l'art social* [The Writer and Social Art], Bibliothèque de l'art social, 1896.

5. Bernard Lazare's political articles were published in the 1890s in daily papers such as the *Écho de Paris*, *Le Voltaire, Paris*, and in the weekly that he created briefly in 1896, *L'Action Social*.

6. The *Entretiens politiques et littéraires* [Political and Literary Interviews] began to appear in 1890. The Symbolist authors Paul Adam and Francis Viélé-Griffin were among its editors.

7. Paris, Léon Chailey, 1894. Reprinted in 1934, 1969, 1982 and in 1990 with a preface by Jean-Denis Bredin, Paris, Les éditions 1900. [In English, translated in 1903, New York, The International Library Publishing.]

8. Brussels, 1896; 2nd augmented version, Paris, Stock, 1897.

9. His first Zionist article was published in *Zion* (a review published in Berlin) with the title "Nécessité d'être soi-même" [The Need to be Yourself].

10. Cf. "La Loi et les congrégations" [The Law and Congregations], *Cahiers de la quinzaine*, august, 1902, p. 207–231.

11. See his letter to Herzl published in *Le Flambeau* in April 1899.

12. On Marx's Judeophobia, see Elisabeth De Fontenay, *Les Figures juives de Marx* [Marx's Jewish Figures], Paris, Éditions Galilée, 1973 and Robert Misrahi, *Marx et la question juive* [Marx and the Jewish Question], Paris, Gallimard, 1972.

13. See for example the chapter on Bernard Lazare in Robert Wistrich's book, *Revolutionary Jews from Marx to Trotsky*, London, Harrap, 1976.

14. On anti-Semitism before "The Affair" see Robert F. Byrnes, Antisemitism in Modern France, New Jersey, Rutgers University Press, 1950 and also Stephen Wilson, Ideology and Experience, Antisemitism in France at the time of the Dreyfus Affair, London, Associated University Presses, 1982.

15. Cf. "La solidarité juive" [Jewish Solidarity] (1890) in *Juifs et antisémites, op. cit.*, pp. 16–17.

16. *Ibid.*, pp. 14–15.

17. See the "Preface" to *Contre l'antisémitisme. Histoire d'une polémique* [Against Anti-Semitism. History of a Polemic], Paris, La Différence, 1983, p. 12.

18. In 1895 and 1896, Bernard Lazare published two articles in the Marxist journal *Le Devenir social* that expressed ideas that were close to something we might call "economic Marxism."

19. On this subject, see the book by Nelly Wilson, *Bernard Lazare, op. cit.*, pp. 105–109.

20. *Anti-Semitism: Its History and Causes*, New York, International Library Publishing Co, 1903, p. 8.

21. *Ibid.*, p. 9.

22. *Ibid.*, p. 275.

23. *Ibid.*, pp. 374–375.

24. His first article on the Affair was published in the newspaper *La Justice* on November 17, 1894 under the title "Le nouveau ghetto" [The New Ghetto]. There is no need to add that Bernard Lazare had not met Herzl at the time and was not aware that he had written a piece under the same title.

25. Cf. Nelly Wilson, *op. cit.*, pp. 161–187.

26. See Bernard Lazare's statements in Robert Gauthier (ed.), "*Dreyfusards*," Paris, Collection Archives, 1965, p. 89.

27. On this subject, see Annie Kriegel, "Aux origines françaises du sionisme: l'affaire Dreyfus" [The French Sources of Zionism: the Dreyfus Affair] in *Les Juifs et le monde moderne*, Éditions du Seuil, 1977, pp. 167–179.

28. On the attitude of Jewish community organizations towards Zionism, see Michael R. Marrus, *Les Juifs à l'époque de l'affaire Dreyfus* [Jews at the Time of the Dreyfus Affair], Paris, Calmann-Lévy, 1972, pp. 279–321.

29. Bernard Lazare's first conferences on Zionism were held before the Russian Jewish students' association. *Le Flambeau*, the first socialist Zionist monthly in French, to which Lazare contributed, was edited by Jacques Bahar, a young North African Jew who had joined the Zionist Congress.

30. Cf. Stephen Lukes, *Emile Durkheim. His Life and Work: A Historical and Critical Study*, London, Penguin Books, 1981, p. 345.

31. On the relationship between art and politics, see Madeleine Rebérioux, "Avant-garde esthétique et avant-garde politique" in *Esthétique et Marxisme*, Paris, UGE 10x18, 1974.

32. Unpublished letter of March 24, 1900. Central Zionist Archives, Jerusalem.

33. See his interview in the British newspaper *The Jewish World* on June 3, 1898, where he states his support for Jewish colonization in Palestine.

34. Cf. "Le Prolétariat Juif devant l'antisémitisme" [Jewish Proletariat in the Face of Anti-Semitism] (1899) in *Juifs et antisémites*, *op. cit.*, p. 137.

35. *Le Fumier de Job* [Job's Dungheap], *op. cit.*, p. 85.

36. See "Le Nationalisme et l'émancipation juive" [Nationalism and Jewish Emancipation] in *Juifs et antisémites*, *op. cit.*, pp. 177–178.

37. Cf. a letter from Bernard Lazare to Herzl in *Le Flambeau*, No. 4, April 1899.

38. "Le Congrès sioniste et le Sultan" [The Zionist Congress and the Sultan], *Pro Armenia*, January 10, 1902.

39. He intended to go to the Zionist Congress in London in 1900 but did not attend. See *Juifs et antisémites*, *op. cit.*, pp. XXIII and 220–222.

40. Cf. "Les Juifs en Roumanie," *Cahiers de la quinzaine*, February 1902, pp. 11–103.

41. Cf. "La Loi et les Congrégations," *Cahiers de la quinzaine*, August 1902, pp. 226–227.

42. In his memoirs, Péguy wrote: "You could say that his final pleasures, while he could still walk, while he was still going, were to come warm himself with us on Thursdays of the Cahiers, or to be more precise, the Thursdays at the Cahiers. He enjoyed speaking with Mr. Sorel. I must say that their discussions were generally flavored with great disillusionment. He had a secret taste, a very pronounced, very deep, almost violent taste for Mr. Sorel. A common taste for disillusionment; of people who won't fall for anything." *Notre jeunesse* [Our Youth] (1910), Paris, Gallimard, 1957, p. 96. We know the post-Dreyfus paths taken by Sorel and Péguy, two of those most disappointed by the Affair. Unfortunately, Lazare's premature disappearance does not allow historians to follow an imaginary trail.

Bibliography

The English titles of the books and articles in Hebrew in this bibliography are as they are translated in the publications themselves. Wherever possible, English references for books and articles in translation that were either originally published in English or are available in English translation have been added for English readers.

Almog, Shmuel. *Nationalism, Zionism, Antisemitism* [in Hebrew]. Jerusalem: Ha-Sifria Ha-Ziyonit, 1992.

Anderson, Benedict. *L'Imaginaire national: Réflexions sur l'origine et l'essor du nationalisme*. Translated by Pierre-Emmanuel Dauzat. Paris: La Découverte, 2002. Originally published as *Imagined Communities: Reflections on the Origin and Spread of Nationalism* (London: Verso, 1983).

Aron, Raymond. *L'Opium des intellectuels*. Paris: Calmann-Lévy, 1955. Translated by Terence Kilmartin as *The Opium of the Intellectuals* (New York: W. W. Norton & Co., 1962).

Attias, Jean-Christophe, and Esther Benbassa. *Israël imaginaire*. Paris, Flammarion, 1998. Translated by Susan Emanuel as *Israel, the Impossible Land* (Palo Alto: Stanford University Press, 2002).

Avnery, Uri. *Israel Without Zionists: A Plea for Peace in the Middle East*. London: Macmillan, 1968.

Baer, Yitzhak. *Galut*. New York: Schocken Books, 1947.

Barnai, Ya'akov. *Historiography and Nationalism* [in Hebrew]. Jerusalem: Magnes, 1995.

Bauer, Otto. *La Question des nationalités et la socialdémocratie*. (2 vol.). Paris: Edi, 1988. Originally published as *Die Nationalitätenfrage und Sozialdemokratie* (Vienna: Verlag der Wiener Volksbuchhandlung, 1924). Translated by Joseph O'Donnell as *The Question of Nationalities and Social Democracy* (Minneapolis: University of Minnesota Press, 2000).

Bechtel, Delphine, Bourel, Dominique, and Le Rider, Jacques, eds. *Max Nordau, 1849–1923*. Paris: Cerf, 1996.

Beit Zvi, Shabtai. *Post-Uganda Zionism in the Crisis of the Shoah* [in Hebrew]. Tel Aviv: Bronfman, 1977. Translated by Ralph Mandel as *Post-Uganda Zionism on Trial* (Tel Aviv: S. B. Beit Zvi, 1991).

Benda, Julien, *La Trahison des clercs*, Paris, Grasset, 1927. Translated by Richard Aldington as *The Treason of the Intellectuals* (New York: William Morrow & Co., 1928).

Ben David, Joseph, "Universities in Israel: Dilemmas of Growth, Diversification, and Administration." In *Education in a Comparative Context: Studies of Israeli Society*, IV. Edited by E. Krausz (New Brunswick: Transaction Publishers, 1989): 148–173.

Ben-Gurion, David, and Yitzhak Ben Zvi. *Eretz Israel in the Past and in the Present* [in Hebrew]. Jerusalem: Yad Ben Zvi, 1979.

Berlin, Isaiah. *À contre-courant*. Translated by André Berelowitch. Paris: Albin Michel, 1988. Originally published as *Against the Current: Essays in the History of Ideas* (London: Hogarth Press, 1979).

Berr, Israel. *Israel's Security: Yesterday, Today, Tomorrow* [in Hebrew]. Tel Aviv: Amikam, 1966.

Birnbaum, Pierre, ed. *La France de l'affaire Dreyfus*. Paris: Gallimard, 1994.

Bishara, Azmi. *The Arabs in Israel*. Gloucestershire: Arris Books, 2003.

Bishara, Azmi. *Checkpoint*, trans. Rashid Akel. Arles: Actes Sud, 2004.

Bloch, Marc, *La Société féodale* (1939–1940). Paris: Albin Michel, 1968. Translated by L. A. Manyon as *The Feudal Society* (London: Routledge, 1961).

Blum, Léon, *Souvenirs sur l'Affaire* (1935). Paris: Gallimard, 1981.

Bober, Arie, ed. *The Other Israel: The Radical Case Against Zionism*. New York: Doubleday Anchor, 1972.

Borochov, Ber. *Works: Volume I* [in Hebrew]. Tel Aviv: Ha-Kibutz Ha-Meuchad, 1955.

Bredin, Jean-Denis. *L'Affaire*. Paris: Julliard, 1983. Translated by Jeffrey Mehlman as *The Affair: The Case of Alfred Dreyfus*. (New York: G. Braziller, 1986).

Carr, Edward H. *Qu'est-ce que l'histoire* (1961). Translated by Maud Sissung. Paris: La Découverte, 1988. Originally published as *What is History?* (1961), revised edition, ed. R.W. Davies (Harmondsworth: Penguin, 1986).

Charle, Christophe. "Champ littéraire et champ du pouvoir: les écrivains et l'affaire Dreyfus." *Annales*, XXXII, no. 2 (1977): 240–264.

Cohen, Uri, *Intellectuals in a National Crystallization Process: The Relationship of the Hebrew University in Jerusalem and the Jewish Settlement in Eretz-Israel, 1925–1948* [in Hebrew, unpublished dissertation]. Hebrew University of Jerusalem, 1996.

Cordova, Avraham. "The Institutionalization of a Cultural Center in Palestine: The Writers' Association." *Jewish Social Studies*, XLII, no. 1 (1980): 37–62.

Cordova, Avraham. "Unsolicited Intellectuals in Politics: The case of Brit Ha-Biryonim." In *Hebrew Literature and the Labor Movement* [in Hebrew], edited by Pinhas Ginossar, 224–242. Beer Sheva: Ben-Gurion University Press, 1989.

Cordova, Avraham, and Hanna Herzog. "The Cultural Endeavor of the Labor Movement in Palestine: A Study of the Relationship between Intelligentsia and

Intellectuals." *Yivo, Annual of Jewish Social Science*, VII (1978): 238–259.

Coser, Lewis A. *Men of Ideas*. New York: Simon & Schuster, 1965.

Debray, Régis. *Le Pouvoir intellectuel en France*. Paris: Ramsay, 1979. Translated by David Macey as *Teachers, Writers, Celebrities: The Intellectuals of Modern France* (London: Verso, 1981).

Diamond, James. *Homeland or Holy Land: The "Canaanite" Critique of Israel*. Indianapolis: Indiana University Press, 1986.

Durkheim, Émile. *La Science sociale et l'action*. Paris: PUF, 1970.

Edelman, Diana V., ed. *The Triumph of Elohim from Yahwism to Judaism*. Michigan: William B. Eerdmans, 1996.

Eisenstadt, Shmuel N. *Israeli Society: Background, Development and Problems* [in Hebrew]. Jerusalem: Magnes, 1967. Published in English as *Israeli Society* (New York: Basic Books, 1967).

Eisenstadt, Shmuel N. *The Transformation of Israeli Society* [in Hebrew]. Jerusalem: Magnes, 1989. Published in English as *The Transformation of Israeli Society: An Essay in Interpretation* (Boulder: Westview Press, 1985).

Ettinger, Shmuel. "Le peuple juif et Eretz Israël." *Les Temps modernes*, 253 bis, (1967): 394–413.

Even Zohar, Itamar. "The Emergence of a Native Hebrew culture in Palestine: 1882–1948." *Studies in Zionism*, IV (1981): 167–184.

Evron, Boas. *A National Reckoning* [in Hebrew]. Tel Aviv: Dvir, 1988. Published in English as *Jewish State or Israeli Nation?* (Bloomington: Indiana University Press, 1995).

Falola, Toyin. *Nationalism and African Intellectuals*. New York: University of Rochester Press, 2001.

Feige, Michael. *One Space, Two Places: "Gush Emunim," "Peace Now" and the Construction of Israeli Space* [in Hebrew]. Jerusalem: Magnes, 2002.

Ferro, Marc. *Comment on raconte l'histoire aux enfants à travers le monde entier*. Paris: Payot, 1981. Translated by Norman Stone and Andrew Brown as *The Use and Abuse of History: Or How the Past Is Taught to Children* (London: Routledge & Kegan Paul, 1984).

Finkelstein, Israel, and Neil Asher Silberman. *La Bible dévoilée: Les nouvelles révélations de l'archéologie*. Translated by Patrice Ghirardi. Paris: Bayard, 2002. Originally published as *The Bible Unearthed: Archaeology's New Vision of Ancient Israel and the Origin of Its Sacred Texts* (New York: Touchstone, 2002).

Flapan, Simha. *The Birth of Israel: Myths and Realities*. New York: Pantheon, 1987.

Foucault, Michel. *Dits et écrits*. Paris: Gallimard, 1976.

Friling, Tuvia, ed. *Critique du post-sionisme: réponse aux "nouveaux historiens" israéliens*. Paris: In Press, 2004.

Furet, François. *Le Passé d'une illusion*. Paris: Robert Laffont/Calmann-Lévy, 1995. Translated by Deborah Furet as *The Passing of an Illusion: The Idea of Communism in the Twentieth Century* (Chicago: University of Chicago Press, 1999).

Gal, Reuven, ed. *The Seventh War: The Effects of the Intifada on the Israeli Society* [in Hebrew]. Tel Aviv: Ha-Kibutz Ha-Meuchad, 1990.

Gellner, Ernest. *Nations et nationalisme.* Translated by Bénédicte Pineau. Paris: Payot, 1989. Originally published as *Nations and Nationalism* (Oxford: Blackwell, 1983).

Gertz, Nurith. *Literature and Ideology in Eretz Israel during the 1930s* [in Hebrew]. Tel Aviv: Open University Press, 1988.

Ginossar, Pinhas and Avi Bareli, eds. *Zionism, A Contemporary Controversy: Research Trends and Ideological Approaches* [in Hebrew]. Beer Sheva: Ben-Gurion University Press, 1996.

Gorny, Yosef. "The Changes in the Social and the Political Structure of the 'Second Alya' in the Years 1904–1940" [in Hebrew]. *Zionut*, I (1970): 205–246.

Gramsci, Antonio. *Écrits politiques: tome I, 1914–1920.* Translated by Marie G. Martin, Gilbert Moget, Armando Tassi, and Robert Paris. Paris: Gallimard, 1974.

Greilsammer, Ilan. *La Nouvelle Histoire d'Israël: Essai sur une identité nationale.* Paris: Gallimard, 1998.

Gresh, Alain. *Israël, Palestine: Vérités sur un conflit.* Paris: Fayard, 2001.

Grodzinsky, Yosef. *Good Human Material* [in Hebrew]. Or Yehuda: Hed Arzi Publishing, 1998. Published in English as *In the Shadow of the Holocaust: The Struggle Between Jews and Zionists in the Aftermath of World War II* (Monroe: Common Courage Press, 2004).

Grossman, David. *Le Vent jaune.* Translated by Suzanne Meron. Paris, Éditions du Seuil, 1988. Translated by Haim Watzman as *The Yellow Wind* (New York: Farrar, Straus and Giroux, 1988).

Hadar-Ramage, Yona, ed. *Thinking It Over: Conflicts in Israeli Public Thought* [in Hebrew]. Ramat Efal: Yad Tabenkin, 1994.

Halamish, Aviva. "Zionist Immigration Policy in the 1930's: From 'Redemption' to 'Survival'" [in Hebrew]. *Zmanim*, XIV, no. 58 (1997): 86–98.

Hazoni, Yoram. *The Jewish State: The Struggle for Israel's Soul.* New York: Basic Books, 2001.

Heller, Joseph. *From Brit Shalom to Ichud: Judah Leib Magnes and the Struggle for Binational State in Palestine* [in Hebrew]. Jerusalem: Magnes, 2003.

Herman, Tamar. *From the "Peace Covenant" to "Peace Now": The Pragmatic Pacifism of the Israeli Peace Camp* [in Hebrew, unpublished doctoral dissertation]. Tel Aviv University, 1989.

Herzl, Theodor. *L'État des Juifs* [Judenstaat]. Translated by Claude Klein. Paris: La Découverte, 2003. Available in English as *The Jewish State* (New York: Dover Publications, 1988).

Hess, Moses. *Rome et Jerusalem.* Paris: Albin Michel, 1981. Originally published as *Rom und Jerusalem, die Letzte Nationalitätsfrage* (Leipzig: Eduard Mengler, 1862). Translated by Maurice J. Bloom as *Rome and Jerusalem* (New York: Philosophical Library, 1958).

Hobsbawm, Eric. *Nations et nationalisme depuis 1780.* Translated by Dominique Peter. Paris: Gallimard, 2001. Originally published as *Nations and Nationalism since 1780: Programme, Myth, Reality* (Cambridge: Cambridge University Press,1990).

Israeli, A. *Peace, Peace, When There Is No Peace* [in Hebrew]. Jerusalem: Bokhan, 1961.

Jabotinsky, Vladimir (Ze'ev). *Exile and Assimilation* [in Hebrew]. Tel Aviv: Saltzman, 1936.

Jabotinsky, Vladimir (Ze'ev). *The Road to a State* [in Hebrew]. Jerusalem: Ari Jabotinsky, 1963.

Jacoby, Russell. *The Last Intellectuals.* New York: Noonday Press, 1989.

Jones, Gareth Stedman. *Languages of Class: Studies in English Working-Class History, 1832–1982.* Cambridge: Cambridge University Press, 1983.

Julliard, Jacques, and Shlomo Sand, eds. *Georges Sorel en son temps.* Paris: Éditions du Seuil, 1985.

Julliard, Jacques, and Michel Winock, ed. *Dictionnaire des intellectuels français.* Paris: Éditions du Seuil, 1996.

Kapeliouk, Amnon. *Rabin, un assassinat politique.* Paris: Le Monde Éditions, 1996.

Karsh, Efraim. *Fabricating Israeli History: "The New Historians,"* London: Frank Cass, 1997.

Kedar, Aaron. "Brith Shalom: Documents and Introduction." *The Jerusalem Quarterly,* XVIII (1981): 55–85.

Kedourie, Elie. *Nationalism* (1961). Oxford: Blackwell, 1993.

Keren, Michael. *Ben-Gurion and the Intellectuals: Power, Knowledge and Charisma.* Illinois: Northern Illinois University Press, 1983.

Keren, Michael. *The Pen and the Sword: Israeli Intellectuals and the Making of a Nation-State.* Boulder: Westview Press, 1989.

Kidron, Peretz, ed. *Refusnik! Les soldats de la conscience en Israël.* Villeurbanne: Golias, 2005. Published in English as *Refusnik!: Israel's Soldiers of Conscience* (New York: Zed Books, 2005).

Kimmerling, Baruch. *Zionism and Territory: The Socio-Territorial Dimensions of the Zionist Politics.* Berkeley: University of California Press, 1983.

Kimmerling, Baruch, ed. *The Israeli State and Society: Boundaries and Frontiers.* Albany: State University of New York Press, 1989.

Kimmerling, Baruch. "Academic History Caught in the Cross Fire: The Case of Israeli–Jewish historiography." *History and Memory,* VII, 1 (1995): 41–65.

Kimmerling, Baruch. *The Invention and Decline of Israeliness. State, Society and the Military.* Berkeley: University of California Press, 2001.

Kimmerling, Baruch. *Immigrants, Settlers, Natives: The Israeli State and Society Between Cultural Pluralism and Cultural Wars* [in Hebrew]. Tel Aviv: Am Oved, 2004.

Kimmerling, Baruch, and Joel Migdal. *Palestinians: The Making of a People.* New York: The Free Press, 1993.

Klein, Menahem. *Bar-Ilan: University Between Religion and Politics* [in Hebrew]. Jerusalem: Magnes, 1998.

Kohn, Hans. *Idea of Nationalism* (1944). New York: Macmillan, 1961.

Konrád, György, and Iván Szelényi. *La Marche au pouvoir des intellectuels.* Translated by Georges Kassai et Pierre Kende. Paris: Éditions du Seuil, 1979.

Koselleck, Reinhart. *Le Futur passé. Contribution à la sémantique des temps historiques.* Translated by Jochen Hoock and Marie-Claire Hoock. Paris, Éditions de l'EHESS, 1990. Originally published as *Vergangene Zukunft: Zur Semantik geschichtlichter Zeiten* (Frankfurt: Suhrkamp Verlag, 1979). Translated by Keith Tribe as *Futures Past: On the Semantics of Historical Time* (Cambridge: MIT Press, 1985).

Kriegel, Annie. *Les Juifs et le monde moderne.* Paris: Éditions du Seuil, 1977.

Laor, Yitzhak. *Things That Are Better (Not) Kept Silent: Essays* [in Hebrew]. Tel Aviv: Babel, 2002.

Lavsky, Hagit. "The Puzzle of Brith Shalom's Impact on the Zionist Polemic during its Time and Afterwards" [in Hebrew]. *Zionut*, XIX (1995): 167–181.

Lissak, Moshe. *The Elites of the Jewish Community in Palestine* [in Hebrew]. Tel Aviv: Am Oved, 1981.

Lissak, Moshe. "'Critical' Sociologists and 'Establishment' Sociologists in the Israeli Academic Community: Ideological Struggles or an Academic Discourse?" *Israel Studies*, I, no. 1 (1996): 247–294.

Lukes, Steven. *Emile Durkheim, His Life and Work: A Historical and Critical Study.* London: Penguin Books, 1981.

Maddy-Weitzman, Bruce. *Palestinian and Israeli Intellectuals in the Shadow of Oslo and Intifadat Al-Aqsa.* Tel Aviv: Dayan Center, 2003.

Marrus, Michael R. *Les Juifs à l'époque de l'affaire Dreyfus.* Translated by Micheline Legras. Paris: Calmann-Lévy, 1972. Originally published as *The Politics of Assimilation: A Study of the French Jewish Community at the Time of the Dreyfus Affair* (Oxford: Clarendon Press, 1971).

Medem, Vladimir. *Fun mayn Lebn—Ma vie.* Translated by Henri Minczeles. Paris: Champion, 1999. Translated by Samuel A. Portnoy as *Vladimir Medem: The Life and Soul of a Legendary Jewish Socialist* (New York: Ktav Pub. House, 1979).

Mendes-Flohr, Paul R., eds. *A Land of Two Peoples: Martin Buber on Jews and Arabs.* New York: Oxford University Press, 1983.

Michael, Reuven. *Heinrich Graetz: The Historian of the Jewish People* [in Hebrew]. Jerusalem: Bialik, 2003.

Minczeles, Henri. *Histoire générale du Bund, un mouvement révolutionnaire juif.* Paris: Denoël, 1999.

Miron, Dan. *When Loners Come Together: A Portrait of Hebrew Literature at the Turn of the Twentieth Century* [in Hebrew]. Tel Aviv: Am Oved, 1970.

Miron, Dan. "From Creators and Builders to Homeless" [in Hebrew]. *Igra: Almanac for Literature and Art*, II (1985–1986.): 106–118.

Miron, Dan. "Document in Israel" [in Hebrew]. *Politika* (August 16, 1987): 37–45.

Morris, Benny. *The Birth of the Palestinian Refugee Problem, 1947–1949.* Cambridge: Cambridge University Press, 1988.

Morris, Benny. "The New Historiography: Israel Confronts its Past." *Tikkun*, IV (1988): 19–23 and 99–102.

Morris, Benny. *Jews and Arabs in Palestine/Israel, 1936–1956* [in Hebrew]. Tel Aviv: Am Oved, 2000.

Morris, Benny. *Victimes: Histoire revisitée du conflit arabo-sioniste.* Bruxelles: Complexe, 2003.

Motyl, Alexander, ed. *Encyclopedia of Nationalism.* London: Academic Press, 2000.

Myers, David N. *Re-Inventing the Jewish Past: European Jewish Intellectuals and Zionist Return to History.* New York: Oxford University Press, 1995.

Nimrod, Yoram. *War or Peace? Formation of Patterns in Israeli Arab Relations, 1947–1950* [in Hebrew]. Givat Haviva: Institute for Peace Studies, 2000.

Noiriel, Gérard. "Socio-histoire d'un concept: les usages du mot "nationalité" au XIXe siècle." In *État, nation et immigration*, 219–247. Paris: Gallimard, 2005.

Nordau, Max. "The History of the Israeli People" [1901, in Hebrew]. In *Zionist Works*, vol. II, 46–50. Jerusalem: Ha-Sifria Ha-Ziyonit, 1960.

Oz, Amos. *In the Land of Israel* [in Hebrew]. Tel Aviv: Am Oved, 1983.

Oz, Amos. *The Slopes of Lebanon* [in Hebrew]. Tel Aviv: Am Oved, 1987.

Oz, Amos. *But These Are Two Different Wars* [in Hebrew]. Tel Aviv: Keter, 2002.

Pappé, Ilan. *Britain and the Arab-Israeli Conflict, 1948–1951.* London: Macmillan, 1988.

Pappé, Ilan. "Critique and Agenda: Post-Zionist Scholars in Israel." In *History and Memory*, VII, no. 1 (1995): 66–90.

Pappé, Ilan. *Une terre pour deux peuples: histoire de la Palestine moderne.* Translated by Odile Demange. Paris: Fayard, 2004. Originally published as *A History of Modern Palestine: One Land, Two Peoples* (Cambridge: Cambridge University Press, 2003).

Pappé, Ilan. *Les Démons de la Nakbah: les libertés fondamentales dans l'université israélienne.* Translated by Marc-Ariel Friedemann. Paris: La Fabrique, 2004. Available in English as *Out of the Frame: The Struggle for Academic Freedom in Israel* (London: Pluto Press, 2010).

Pawel, Ernst. *Theodor Herzl ou le Labyrinthe de l'exil.* Translated by Françoise Adelstain. Paris: Éditions du Seuil, 1992. Originally published as *The Labyrinth of Exile: A Life of Theodor Herzl* (New York: Farrar, Straus & Giroux, 1989).

Pinsker, Leon. *Auto-Emancipation* [in Hebrew]. Jerusalem: Ha-Istadrut Ha-Ziyonit, 1962. Translated by Dr. D.S. Blondheim as *Auto-Emancipation* (New York: Zionist Organization of America, 1948).

Piterberg, Gabriel. "The Nation and its Raconteurs: *Orientalism* and nationalist historiography" [in Hebrew]. *Theory and Criticism*, VI (1995): 81–103.

Porath, Yehoshua. *The Emergence of the Palestinian–Arab Movement* [in Hebrew]. Tel Aviv: Am Oved, 1976.

Ram, Uri. "Zionist Historiography and the Invention of Modern Jewish Nationhood: The Case of Ben Zion Dinur." *History and Memory*, VII, no. 1 (1995): 91–124.

Raz-Krakotzkin, Amnon. *The National Narration of Exile: Zionist Historiography and Medieval Jewry* [in Hebrew, unpublished doctoral dissertation]. Tel Aviv University, 1996.

Rein, Ariel. "History and Jewish History: Together or Separate? The Definition of Historical Studies at the Hebrew University, 1925–1935" [in Hebrew]. In *The History of the Hebrew University of Jerusalem: Origins and Beginnings* [in Hebrew], ed. Shaul Katz et Michael Heyd, 516–540. Jerusalem: Magnes, 1997.

Rémi-Giraud, Sylvianne and Pierre Rétat, eds. *Les Mots de la nation*. Lyon: Presses universitaires de Lyon, 1996.

Rinot, Moshe. "The Struggle between the Teacher's Union and the Zionist Organization for Hegemony in Hebrew Education in Palestine" [in Hebrew], *Zionut*, IV (1975): 114–145.

Rogan, Eugene L., and Avi Shlaim, eds. *La Guerre de Palestine, 1948: derrière le mythe*. Paris: Autrement, 2002.

Ruppin, Arthur. *The Social Structure of the Jews* [in Hebrew]. Berlin/Tel Aviv: Shtibel, 1934.

Saïd, Edward W. *L'Orientalisme: l'Orient créé par l'Occident*. Translated by Catherine Malamoud. Paris: Éditions du Seuil, 1980. Originally published as *Orientalism* (New York: Pantheon, 1978).

Sand, Shlomo. "Jean Jaurès et la question nationale." *Pluriel-débat*, XII (1977): 31–52.

Sand, Shlomo. *L'Illusion du politique: Georges Sorel et le débat intellectuel 1900*. Paris: La Découverte, 1984.

Sand, Shlomo. "Sorel, les juifs et l'antisémitisme." *Cahiers Georges Sorel*, II (1984): 7–36.

Sand, Shlomo. "Mirror, Mirror on the Wall, Who Is the True Intellectual of Them All? Self-image of the Intellectual in France." In *Intellectuals in Twentieth-Century France*, ed. Jeremy Jennings, 33–58. London: Macmillan, 1993.

Sand, Shlomo. "Le marxisme et les intellectuels vers 1900." In *Jaurès et les intellectuels*, ed. Madeleine Rebérioux and Gilles Candar, 203–222. Paris: L'Atelier, 1994.

Sand, Shlomo. *Les Intellectuels, la vérité et le pouvoir* [in Hebrew]. Tel Aviv: Am Oved, 2000.

Sand, Shlomo. "A Flirt or a Love Affair? French Intellectuals between Fascism and Nazism." In *The Development of the Radical Right in France*, ed. Edward J. Arnold, 83–99. London: Macmillan, 2000.

Sand, Shlomo. *Le XXe siècle à l'écran*. Paris: Éditions du Seuil, 2004.

Sartre, Jean-Paul. *Plaidoyer pour les intellectuels*. Paris: Gallimard, 1972. Translated by John Matthews as "A Plea for Intellectuals" in *Between Existentialism and Marxism* by Jean-Paul Sartre, 228–285. New York: Pantheon, 1974.

Scott, James M., ed. *Exile: Old Testament, Jewish, and Christian Conceptions*. Leyden: Brill, 1997.

Schweid, Eliezer. *The World of A.D. Gordon* [in Hebrew]. Tel Aviv: Am Oved, 1970.

Segev, Tom. *Le Septième Million*. Translated by Eglal Errera. Paris: Liana Levi, 1993. Translated by Haim Watzman as *The Seventh Million: The Israelis and the Holocaust* (New York: Hill and Wang, 1993).

Shafir, Gershon. *Land, Labor and the Origins of the Israeli-Palestinian Conflict, 1882–1914*. Cambridge: Cambridge University Press, 1989.

Shaham, Nathan, and Zvi Raanan, eds. *War in the Gulf: Collection of Essays* [in Hebrew]. Tel Aviv: Sifriat Poalim, 1991.

Shammas, Anton. *Arabesques*. Translated by Guy Séniak. Arles: Actes Sud, 1988. Translated by Vivian Eden as *Arabesques: A Novel* (New York: Harpercollins, 1988).

Shapira, Anita. "Politics and Collective Memory: The Debate over the New Historians in Israel." *History and Memory*, VII, no. 1 (1995): 9–40.

Shapira, Anita, and Derek J. Penslar, eds. *Israeli Historical Revisionism: From Left to Right*. London: Frank Cass, 2002.

Shapira, Yonathan. *An Elite Without Successors: Generations of Political Leaders in Israel* [in Hebrew]. Tel Aviv: Sifriat Poalim, 1984.

Shavit, Ari, ed. *Partition: Disengagement and Beyond* [in Hebrew]. Tel Aviv: Keter, 2005.

Shavit, Zohar. *The Literary Life in Eretz Israel 1910–1933* [in Hebrew]. Tel Aviv: Ha-Kibutz Ha-Meuchad, 1982.

Shenhav, Yehouda. *The Arab-Jews: Nationalism, Religion and Ethnicity* [in Hebrew]. Tel Aviv: Am Oved, 2003. Translated into English as *The Arab Jew: A Postcolonial Reading of Nationalism, Religion, and Ethnicity* (Stanford: Standford University Press, 2006).

Shils, Edward. "The Intellectuals in the Political Development of the New States." *World Politics*, XII, no. 3 (1960): 329–368.

Shils, Edward. *The Intellectuals and the Powers and Other Essays*. Chicago: University of Chicago Press, 1972.

Shlaim, Avi. *Collusion Across the Jordan: King Abdullah, the Zionist Movement and the Partition of Palestine*. Oxford: Oxford University Press, 1988.

Shohat, Ella. *Israeli Cinema, East/West and the Politics of Representation*. Austin: University of Texas Press, 1989.

Silberstein, Laurence J. *The Postzionism Debates: Knowledge and Power in Israeli Culture*. New York: Routledge, 1999.

Vidal-Naquet, Pierre. "Dreyfus dans l'Affaire et dans l'histoire." In *Les Juifs, la mémoire et le présent*, vol. II, 88–128. Paris: La Découverte, 1991.

Vrubel-Golubkina, Irena, and Nir Baram, eds. *Contemporary Russian Literature in Israeli Discourse* [in Hebrew]. Tel Aviv: Am Oved, 2005.

Weinstock, Nathan. *Le Pain de misère: Histoire du mouvement ouvrier juif en Europe*, vol. I. Paris: La Découverte, 1984.

Weitz, Yechiam, ed. *From Vision to Revision: A Hundred Years of Historiography of Zionism* [in Hebrew]. Jerusalem: Zalman Shazar, 1997.

Werblowsky, R.J. Zwi. "Israël et Eretz Israël." *Les Temps modernes*, 253 bis (1967): 371–393.

Wexler, Paul. *The Schizoid Nature of Modern Hebrew: A Slavic Language in Search of a Semitic Past.* Wiesbaden: Otto Harrassowitz, 1991.

Yiftachel, Oren. "Ethnocracy: The Politics of Judaizing Israel/Palestine." *Constellation*, no. 6 (1999): 364–390.

Zertal, Idith. *Des rescapés pour un État: la politique sioniste d'émigration clandestine en Palestine, 1945–1948.* Translated by Jacqueline Carnaud and Jacqueline Lahana. Paris: Calmann-Lévy, 2000. Translated into English as *Catastrophe and Power: Holocaust Survivors and the Emergence of Israel* (Berkeley: University of California Press, 1998).

Zertal, Idith. *La Nation et la Mort: la Shoah dans le discours et la politique d'Israël.* Translated by Marc Saint-Upéry. Paris: La Découverte, 2004. Translated by Chaya Galai as *Israel's Holocaust and the Politics of Nationhood* (Cambridge: Cambridge University Press, 2005).

Zuckermann, Moshe. *Shoah in the Sealed Room: The "Holocaust" in Israeli Press During the Gulf War* [in Hebrew]. Tel Aviv: private printing, 1993.

Index

Machover, Moshe, 215n2
Maddy-Weitzman, Bruce, 209n40, 226
Magnes, Judah L., 59, 207n21, 224
Major, John, 148
Marrus, Michael R., 219n28, 226
Marx, Karl, 14, 18, 19, 30, 46, 115,
    144, 185, 189, 218
Maurras, Charles, 40
Medem, Vladimir, 49, 206n5, 226
Meged, Aaron, 63
Meir, Golda, 14, 53
Mendes-Flohr, Paul R., 207n20, 226
Michael, Reuven, 205n16, 226
Michael, Sami, 84, 96
Migdal, Joel, 170, 216n17, 225
Minczeles, Henri, 206n4, 226
Miron, Dan, 135, 136, 206n7,
    208n24, 208n31, 226
Mommsen, Theodor, 36, 39
Morin, Edgar, 135
Morris, Benny, 92, 93, 156, 160, 162,
    165, 166, 210n52, 214n1,
    215n1, 216n11, 227
Motyl, Alexander, 27, 204n6, 227
Moussa, Mahmoud, 10
Mussolini, Benito, 17–19, 141
Myers, David N., 217n19, 227

Napoleon I (Napoleon Bonaparte), 126
Nasser, Gamal Abdel, 141, 153
Ne'eman, Yehuda, 74
Netanyahu, Benjamin, 81, 84, 85, 95
Nimrod, Yoram, 216n10, 227
Noiriel, Gérard, 211n2, 227
Nordau, Max, 46, 112, 205n1, 212n10,
    221, 227

Orpaz, Yitzhak, 149
Orr, Akiva, 215n2
Orwell, George, 100
Oz, Amos, 67, 70, 73, 79, 87, 90, 95,
    104, 127, 146–148, 210n50,
    213n21, 227

Pappé, Ilan, 156, 160–162, 165, 166,
    214n1, 215n7, 215n10, 227
Pascal, Blaise, 180
Pawel, Ernst, 204n10, 227
Péguy, Charles, 181, 201, 220n42
Peled, Mattityahu, 154
Penn, Alexander, 54
Penslar, Derek J., 216n12, 229
Peres, Shimon, 79, 94
Philippe II d'Espagne, 141, 152
Pinsker, Leon, 122, 212n16, 227
Piterberg, Gabriel, 215n8, 227
Plato, 12
Pontecorvo, Gillo, 22
Porath, Yehoshua, 119, 122, 212n14,
    227

Raanan, Zvi, 213n5, 229
Rabikovitch, Daliah, 96
Rabin, Yitzhak, 77–80, 84–86, 127,
    179, 209n36, 209n40, 225
Ram, Uri, 161, 175–177, 217n19, 228
Ratosh, Yonathan, 60
Raz-Krakotzkin, Amnon, 217n21, 228
Réberioux, Madeleine, 14, 203n7,
    222, 228
Rein, Ariel, 215n3, 228
Rémi-Giraud, Sylvianne, 211n2, 228
Renan, Ernest, 40, 41, 155, 205n16
Resnais, Alain, 22
Rétat, Pierre, 211n2, 228
Revel, Jacques, 20
Rinot, Moshe, 207n18, 228
Robespierre, Maximilien de, 19
Rogan, Eugene L., 216n10, 228
Rolland, Romain, 135, 154
Rotenstreich, Nathan, 63
Rousseau, Jean-Jacques, 19
Ruppin, Arthur, 112, 212n10, 228

Sadan, Dov, 68
Saïd, Edward W., 215n8, 228
Sartre, Jean-Paul, 26, 204n2, 228

Acknowledgments

I would like to express my thanks to all those who helped me see this book through to publication.

I would also like to take this opportunity to thanks my students at Tel-Aviv University. Our discussions helped me determine the many gray and "forbidden" areas of Zionist and Israeli history. I hope that some of them will continue to explore these new areas of research and pursue some of the directions that I proposed to them.

As for my wife Varda and my two daughters Edith and Liel, I owe them so much more than words can express.

A condensed version of the first chapter of this book was published in Shlomo Sand, *Intellectuals, Truth and Power* (in Hebrew), Tel-Aviv, Am Oved, 2000, p. 62–75 (and in English in Jeremy Jennings and Anthony Kemp Welch (dir.), *Intellectuals in Politics. From the Dreyfus Affair to Salman Rushdie*, London, Routledge, 1997, p. 102–119).

The second chapter of this work corresponds to chapter VI of Shlomo Sand, *Intellectuals, Truth and Power*, op. cit., p. 174–202.

The third chapter of the present work was published in Shlomo Sand, *Intellectuals, Truth and Power*, op. cit., p. 203–222, and in *Matériaux pour l'histoire de notre temps*, 48, 1997, pp. 46–51.

The fourth chapter of the present work appeared in *Annales. Histoire, Sciences sociales*, 1, 59th year, 2004, p. 143–160 and was included in Shlomo Sand, *Historians, Time and Imagination* (in Hebrew), Tel-Aviv, Am Oved, 2004, p. 96–118.